Subject Access to
Visual Resources Collections

Recent Titles in
New Directions in Information Management

SUBJECT ACCESS TO VISUAL RESOURCES COLLECTIONS

A Model for Computer Construction
of Thematic Catalogs

KAREN MARKEY

NEW DIRECTIONS IN INFORMATION MANAGEMENT, NUMBER 11

GREENWOOD PRESS
New York · Westport, Connecticut · London

13015

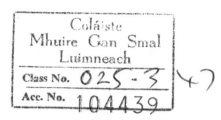
Library of Congress Cataloging-in-Publication Data

Markey, Karen.
  Subject access to visual resources collections.
  (New directions in information management,
ISSN 0887–3844 ; no. 11)
  Bibliography: p.
  Includes index.
  1. Cataloging of pictures—Data processing.
2. Cataloging of art—Data processing. 3. Cataloging
of non-book materials—Data processing. 4. Subject
cataloging—Data processing. 5. Audio-visual library
service—Data processing. 6. Information storage
and retrieval systems—Art. I. Title. II. Series.
Z699.5.P53M37 1986   025.3'47   86–7658
ISBN 0–313–24031–0 (lib. bdg. : alk. paper)

Library of Congress Catalog Card Number: 86–7658
ISBN: 0–313–24031–0
ISSN: 0887–3844

First published in 1986

Greenwood Press, Inc.
88 Post Road West, Westport, Connecticut 06881

Printed in the United States of America

The paper used in this book complies with the
Permanent Paper Standard issued by the National
Information Standards Organization (Z39.48–1984).

10 9 8 7 6 5 4 3 2 1

For my mother

Contents

Figures

Tables

Preface

Research conducted at the School of Information Studies of Syracuse University served as the foundation for this book. In that research, completed in 1981, I found that the identification of subject matter in iconographical research collections was familiar only to iconographers and others who knew the symbolic meaning of the representational elements in artworks. I tested a method for developing a subject searching aid to iconographical research collections in which individuals who were untrained in iconography could translate their inquiry into the appropriate symbolic theme or concept and then search the iconographical research collection at hand. The results of the test were a prototype searching aid, recommendations for refining the searching aid and enlisting it as a tool for searchers of existing iconographical research collections, and suggestions about how the aid could become an online search tool to access databases of iconographical research collections.

In this book, the method of developing a subject searching aid has been generalized to include a wide variety of visual resources collections, such as slide collections in museum or university fine arts departments; picture collections and vertical files in public libraries; public or personal collections of picture postcards, photographs, or postage stamps; photographs in magazine or newspaper morgues; and original artifacts in museums and art galleries.

A method for describing subject matter in visual images is

based on Erwin Panofsky's study of meaning in the visual arts. The method was tested using photographic reproductions of works of art from the late medieval period in Northern European painting.

This book provides a step-by-step approach for describing subject content in visual images and compiling a tool to aid searchers of a visual resources collection to find images of interest. This searching tool—a thematic catalog of primary and secondary subject matter—allows users of a visual resources collection who do not have the specialized knowledge required to search specialized visual resources collections effectively to translate their search inquiry into the terminology of the specialized collection.

In September 1984, the Second International Conference on Automatic Processing of Art History Data and Documents sponsored by the Scuola Normale Superiore (Pisa) and The J. Paul Getty Trust (Los Angeles) was held at the Scuola in Pisa, Italy. Oral remarks by conference participants and presenters centered on comparing subject searching tools to determine the best one. These remarks demonstrated the need for a review of the major methods of subject access to visual resources collections. The review presented in this book can be used to characterize methods of subject access to existing visual resources collections, recognize the methods' strengths and weaknesses, and make more accurate comparisons or appraisals than those comparisons that consider only topical, geographical and chronological coverage.

Books and research are cooperative endeavors. Although one person is responsible for the research and writing, the author depends on and benefits from many others for ideas, criticism, and support. I am most indebted to a number of people and wish to express my sincere thanks to them.

My earliest ideas about this research were shaped and directed by exploratory projects and conversations with Harold Cole, David Penniman, and Jeffrey Katzer. Johanna Prins and Ingeborg Wald allowed me to select images from their slide collections at Syracuse University and Cornell University, respectively. Wald also helped me recruit iconographers in the Department of Art History to take part in the experiment. Gerard Salton of Cornell

University generously provided me with a copy of an overlapping clustering algorithm and access to his students Elena Seifrid, Harry Wu, and Ed Fox, who answered my many questions about the algorithm. Michael Stratoti helped me install the algorithm on the Syracuse computer.

Pauline A. Cochrane of Syracuse University deserves special thanks for suggesting that I pursue research of personal interest and encouraging me to collect, analyze, and interpret original data. Friends and colleagues provided helpful criticism and were themselves sources of information, particularly Constance Joseph, Todd Weseloh, and Lenore Sarasan. Virginia Voedisch helped immensely in editing the manuscript of the book. Text entry of the book was provided by Cindy Heffelfinger.

Published information on subject access to visual resources collections is scattered in many different and unrelated publications. Since 1978 over a half-dozen conferences organized to gather the keepers of visual resources collections have generated more published information on various collections activities and projects and more information in convenient sources. Furthermore, these conferences have identified a need for standards for describing visual resources collections; however, up-to-date and accurate research about visual resources collections is lacking. There is no research to answer such questions about who uses visual resources collections, how often and for what purpose they use these collections, what types of questions they intend to answer by consulting these collections, what types of queries they present to these collections, and what the functions of these collections are. Answers to such questions are critical at this time when manual searching tools are being converted to computerized tools and standards for describing visual resources collections are being seriously discussed.

The research in this book increases our knowledge about how scholars in the history of art and untrained indexers describe and access the subject matter of works of art. A gold mine of answers to questions about the use and users of visual resources collections is as yet untapped.

Introduction

All of us are familiar with the phrase, "A picture is worth a thousand words." That phrase underlines the ease with which the visual image conveys its meaning and the corresponding difficulty of using words to describe, reconstruct, or replace the visual image. Visual images range from the abstract—a mental image of a personal experience—to the concrete—a pictorial image captured by a photographic medium. Expressing the visual image in words is a difficult and often frustrating effort regardless of the physical format of the image.

Yet we rely on words to represent visual images for tasks such as organizing a personal slide or photograph collection. Think about how people organize personal photographs. Some might treat each photograph individually, using a list of subject headings and/or a classification scheme. Probably most people leave their slides in the paper folders or plastic boxes that are used as packaging by the processing facility and label this packaging with phrases intended to jog memory about contents, such as "Christmas vacation in Florida" or "Trip to New Guinea." One of my colleagues—a world traveler and avid amateur photographer—merely sticks her photos in a shoebox with no apparent order whatsoever; trying to find a certain picture is a frustrating task because she has to scan nearly every photograph in every shoebox to find the right one.

Words can be employed to help access and retrieve items from a visual image collection. In this book, I introduce a method for describing visual images to aid searchers, regardless of their background and training, in accessing and retrieving images. For the most part, I will treat visual images that are captured by photographic media and artifacts that themselves bear visual images, such as painting or sculpture. The importance of the method covered here is threefold:

1. The method can help searchers of a specialized collection of visual images access that collection without requiring them to be experts in the specialized area that the collection illustrates and upon which it is organized and described by an expert.

2. It enhances access to the subject content of visual images to complement traditional approaches to describing subject content that have been constrained by the available technology for information storage and retrieval, such as precoordinate indexing and manual file storage.

3. It offers a method of describing visual images with a minimum of expenditure by subject specialists and keeps pace with new technological advances in image storage, such as optical disks and micrographics, upon which can be stored thousands of visual images.

The method for describing subject matter in visual images covered in this book is based on a theoretical discussion on the study of meaning or subject matter in art by the late renowned art historian Erwin Panofsky. The method has been tested utilizing photographic reproductions of works of art from the late medieval period in Northern European painting. Such reproductions are typically gathered into large files of photographic reproductions called iconographical research collections, which are accessed by scholars in art history, iconography, medieval studies, and theology. The method and the benefits accruing from the method, however, are not limited to this period of artistic production or this type of visual image collection. The method could be used to describe many different collections of visual images in diverse organizations, including picture collections and vertical file materials at public libraries, picture postcards, representations on postal stamps, photographs in magazine and newspaper morgues, photographic archives in historical societies, and original artifacts in museums and art galleries.

The construction of a thematic catalog of primary and secondary subject matter is the focus of this book. Chapter 1 discusses Erwin Panofsky's theoretical framework upon which the method of describing subject matter in visual images is based. A step-by-step approach to constructing the thematic catalog to visual resources collections using this method of describing subject matter is highlighted in chapter 2. This searching tool—a thematic catalog of primary and secondary subject matter—allows users of a visual images collection who do not have the specialized knowledge required to search specialized visual image collections effectively to translate their search inquiry into the terminology of the specialized collection. The results of compiling a thematic catalog of primary and secondary subject matter using the method described are presented in chapter 3. The chapter also presents the intermediate results of selected steps of this process. The thematic catalog that results from the experiment is featured in chapter 4. In chapter 5, the thematic catalog of primary and secondary subject matter is placed in the perspective of other approaches to describing subject matter in existing collections of visual images. The thematic catalog is one of many approaches to describing subject matter, which can be characterized by three factors: type of subject matter described, method of subject access, and indexing technique. The book concludes with recommendations for providing online computerized display and retrieval of primary subject matter descriptions and the thematic catalog.

Chapter 5 deals with the wide spectrum of types of subject matter, methods of subject access, and subject indexing techniques currently featured by manual and computerized subject catalogs to visual resources collections. In chapter 5, accessing subject matter in existing visual resources collections is featured to enable one to characterize access methods used in visual resources collections of interest and understand each method's strengths and weaknesses. Primary subject matter and the thematic catalog are included in this discussion to place them in the context of existing methods of subject access to visual resources collections and to show how the thematic catalog and primary subject matter can overcome weaknesses of existing subject access methods. Online, computerized retrieval and display of primary subject matter and secondary subject matter is envisioned in a database of information on a visual resources collection and primary and secondary subject matter in a thematic catalog.

Subject Access to
Visual Resources Collections

1 Primary Subject Matter Descriptions for Visual Images

1.1 PANOFSKY AND THE STUDY OF MEANING IN THE VISUAL ARTS

The theoretical framework Erwin Panofsky developed to characterize the study of subject matter or meaning in the visual arts served as an inspiration for devising a method to describe subject matter in visual images. Panofsky (1955;1962) broke down the process of studying subject matter or meaning in the visual arts into three successive levels: (1) preiconographical description, (2) iconographical analysis, and (3) iconological interpretation.

Following the chain of events in these three levels will show how visual images are perceived and understood by the observer. An event takes place when we view and interpret a visual image, particularly a work of art, which Panofsky describes as the "apprehension of significant form." He did not assign a level to the apprehension of significant form, but it is a necessary step in the process of the observer's perception and understanding of a visual image.

Panofsky (1955, 26) used the example of the everyday occurrence of meeting an acquaintance along the street to explain the three levels of interpretation of his scheme. Preiconographical description entails the following operation:

When an acquaintance greets me on the street by lifting his hat, what I see from a formal point of view is nothing but the change of certain details within a configuration forming part of the general pattern of color, lines and volumes which constitutes my world of vision.

As soon as pure visible forms are linked to their corresponding objects, events, or expressional qualities, the viewer has reached the first level. The example of meeting an acquaintance continues along the lines of preiconographical description (Panofsky, 1955, 26):

When I identify, as I automatically do, this configuration as an *object* (gentleman), and the change of detail as an *event* (hat lifting), I have already overstepped the limits of purely formal perception and entered the first sphere of subject matter or meaning. . . . Psychological nuances will invest the gestures of my acquaintance with a further meaning which we shall call *expressional*. (Italics added)

At this first level of interpretation, only knowledge acquired from practical experience is necessary; that is, the viewer merely applies the knowledge and skills used for day-to-day living. Viewers who grasp the significance of the gesture as one of polite greeting have already proceeded from the first level, preiconographical description, to the second, iconographical analysis, in interpreting what might be termed an outdated custom but one still somewhat familiar to those with a knowledge of Western European culture. The example clarifies iconographical analysis (Panofsky, 1955, 27):

Neither an Australian bushman nor an ancient Greek could be expected to realize that the lifting of a hat is not only a practical event with certain expressional connotations, but also a sign of politeness. To understand this significance of the gentleman's action I must not only be familiar with the practical world of objects and events, but with the . . . customs and cultural traditions peculiar to a certain civilization.

Competence in making an iconographical analysis of hat lifting can be achieved through knowledge and understanding of literary sources. The Australian bushman who wishes to decipher the gesture of hat lifting may ultimately rely on a descriptive account in a manual of mid-twentieth century European etiquette, just as the iconographical specialist of thirteenth-century French sculpture consults extant literary sources and religious documents.

The third level, iconological interpretation, requires knowledge beyond mere familiarity with written sources. In the example, the act of hat lifting is viewed as "the basic attitude of a nation, a period, a class, a religious or philosophical persuasion" (Panofsky, 1955, 30). Above all, iconological interpretation requires the art historian to possess "synthetic intuition, i.e., familiarity with the essential tendencies of the human mind" (Panofsky, 1955, 41).

Panofsky enumerates the three levels of interpretation in a synoptic table, which simplifies the descriptive discourse by listing and defining side by side the three levels and their respective objects of interpretation, necessary equipment that observers must possess for interpretation, and corrective principles of interpretation (table 1.1).

1.2 SECONDARY SUBJECT MATTER FOR DESCRIBING VISUAL IMAGES

At present, visual images are described for their secondary subject matter, that is, the second level of interpretation in the visual arts. For example, reproductions in iconographical research collections are assigned subject headings or organized into categories that describe the overall theme or concept represented in the picture. When a reproduction is assigned a subject heading such as "Agony in the Garden" (that is, one that describes the work's secondary subject matter), a collection user who knows the biblical account of the Agony in the Garden has a general idea of the primary subject matter depicted in the work. Undoubtedly a praying Christ, an outdoor scene, and possibly at least three sleeping disciples are represented in "Agony in the Garden." Similarly picture collections in public libraries are assigned subject headings that describe their overall theme. When a picture is assigned a subject heading such as "Drought—Central Ohio—1983" to describe the work's secondary subject matter, a user of this collection who knows of the U.S. Midwest's dry summer of 1983 has a general idea of the primary subject matter depicted in the work. Probably the parched earth and brown corn stalks are still under a blazing sun in this picture.

In both examples, the indexer or picture specialist who described the secondary subject matter of the images and recorded it with a subject heading, annotation, or classification code first had to identify the primary subject matter of the images. Pan-

Table 1.1
Levels of Interpretation in the Visual Arts

	1. Pre-Iconographical Description	2. Iconographical Analysis	3. Iconological Interpretation
Levels of Interpretation	1. Pre-Iconographical Description	2. Iconographical Analysis	3. Iconological Interpretation
Object of Intrepretation	Primary or Natural Subject Matter – (a) factual, (b) expressional – constituting the world of artistic motifs	Secondary or Conventional Subject Matter, constituting the world of images, stories, and allegories	Intrinsic Meaning or Content, constituting the world of "symbolical" values
Equipment for Interpretation	Practical Experience (familiarity with objects and events)	Knowledge of Literary Sources (familiarity with specific themes and concepts)	Synthetic Intuition (familiarity with the essential tendencies of the human mind), conditioned by personal psychology and "Weltanschauung"
Corrective Principle of Interpretation	History of Style (insight into the manner in which, under varying historical conditions, objects and events were expressed by forms)	History of Types (insight into the manner in which, under varying historical conditions, specific themes or concepts were expressed by objects and events)	History of Cultural Symptoms or "symbols in general" (insight into the manner in which, under varying historical conditions, essential tendencies of the human mind were expressed by specific themes and concepts)

SOURCE: Erwin Panofsky, Meaning in the Visual Arts (Garden City, NY: Doubleday Anchor Books, 1955), pp. 40–41.

ofsky's synoptic table of the levels of interpretation in the visual arts shows that preiconographical description (in which primary subject matter is identified) is a prerequisite to iconographical analysis (in which secondary subject matter is identified). The obvious question is, then, why collections of visual images have been described for their secondary subject matter instead of primary subject matter.

The chief reason is that the physical format of collections of visual images—card files or catalogs—precludes the assignment of more than a few subject headings, descriptors, or classification codes to a single visual image. Primary subject matter requires the identification of many entities represented in an image: its objects, events, and expressional qualities. Prior to the introduction of online information storage and retrieval, the physical format of the devices for accessing images was unable to support more than a few entries representing an image's subject matter. The solution has been to apply a vocabulary to represent the overall theme or concept of the visual image—that is, its secondary subject matter.

Thus, secondary subject matter, which by definition constitutes "the world of images, stories, and allegories" (Panofsky, 1955, 41), or the themes and concepts of these images, has been used to describe most collections of visual images. Many of these collections have been established to support scholarly research; thus, secondary subject matter is in accordance with the training and knowledge of the users of such collections. Therefore collections of visual images have been described for their secondary subject matter because such descriptions are well suited to the physical formats of the collections and support the scholarly pursuits of their users.

1.3 ADVANTAGES OF PRIMARY SUBJECT MATTER

Objectivity of interpretation decreases as one proceeds from the representational to thematic—The more we try to unravel in depth the meaning of a symbol, the more complex is the approach, and the greater is the margin of misinterpretation.

This quotation by Wittkower (1955, 117) serves as a caveat that the probability of error is greater in collections whose secondary subject matter is described than those whose primary subject matter is described because the indexer has carried out a process that requires two steps and becomes increasingly subjective as it proceeds beyond the first level of interpretation. According to Panofsky's scheme, iconographical analysis cannot be attained without the identification of primary subject matter (see table 1.1). Thus there is good reason to believe that systems arranged according to secondary subject matter entail more decision making on the part of indexers since they must carry their analyses through two levels. In comparison, the identification of primary subject matter entails analysis at only the first level.

Iconographical analysis involves loss of crucial information since subject headings are generic and compact. For example, one wonders about a scene assigned the secondary subject heading "Madonna and Child." Is the Madonna seated in a regal fashion or standing in a niche-like enclosure? Does the Child gaze toward the viewer or turn affectionately toward his mother? Seemingly moot points, such information is important for the history of types. Lindsay (1968, 33) highlights the fact that iconographical analysis eliminates useful information and employs the Decimal Index to Art of the Low Countries (1961) as an example:

If the researcher is interested in pictorial representations of snakes in the seventeenth century, he will consult the index and find: "snake(s), see also serpent." Under these headings he will be directed to pictures showing *Aaron's staff changed into a serpent, Cadmus and Harmonia changed into a snake*, to name a few, but he will not be directed to depictions of the *Fall of Man* (which contain serpents) or other types of pictures in which snakes are included.

To find representations of snakes, searchers of a collection of visual images accessible through their secondary subject matter must secure in their minds a return to the first level of interpretation (preiconographical description). In this way, they can conjure up entities of preiconographical description, such as the snakes in Lindsay's example, that are subsumed by iconographical analysis and then figure out what secondary subject headings include depictions of snakes.

Anyone searching a collection of visual images accessible by secondary subject matter is at the mercy of the indexer's interpretation. Not only may searchers be biased by the indexer's interpretation of secondary subject matter, but they may spend time proving (to themselves, at least) that the interpretation is wrong, or they may perpetuate the indexer's mistake. Gombrich (1972) demonstrated how the theme of the Angel Raphael and her emblem Tobias had been repeatedly misinterpreted as the theme of Tobias and the angel. Thus, a searcher for this theme would have to check under two headings when searching a collection whose secondary subject matter has been identified and make a learned judgment as to the identity of the theme and its characters. A preiconographical description withholds the identification of Tobias and the angel, however, leaving the analysis of secondary meaning to the searcher.

Novices or unsophisticated searchers are neither sufficiently experienced with iconographical analysis nor familiar with the method to access collections of visual images organized according to secondary subject matter. But to access such collections, these searchers must be familiar with secondary meaning. Requesting pictures of snakes is not good enough; searchers must know themes and concepts that include snakes, such as the Fall of Man and Laocoon. Providing access to collections by primary subject matter can ease the task of searchers since it requires only one level of interpretation, practical experience, and knowledge of the history of style.

Just as searchers of collections of visual images whose primary subject matter is described do not have to have knowledge of secondary subject matter, indexers of such collections do not have to possess such knowledge, which typically takes years of training and study to acquire.

In summary, describing visual images according to their primary subject matter has these advantages:

1. Primary subject matter requires correct interpretation of subject matter at only one level, whereas iconographical analysis presupposes correct identification of primary and secondary subject matter.
2. Secondary subject matter entails the loss of potentially useful information.

3. Users of collections accessible by their secondary subject matter could be biased by the interpretation provided.

4. The task of searchers who are unfamiliar with secondary subject matter is eased by providing access by preiconographical description, which requires only practical experience and knowledge of the history of style.

5. Highly skilled and trained indexers are not needed to identify primary subject matter.

1.4   USES OF PRIMARY SUBJECT MATTER

Generally collections of visual images are accessible only to searchers who have knowledge of iconography or secondary subject matter because secondary subject matter has been used to describe these collections of visual images. An example of iconographical research collections will illustrate this point.

Centers of documentation have developed research collections of reproductions of works of art to aid scholars pursuing iconographical studies, including the Index of Christian Art at Princeton University and the Decimal Index to Art in the Low Countries compiled at the Netherlands Institute of Art History at The Hague. The subject matter of works of art contained in these iconographical research collections has been described along the lines of its symbolic implications so that the ability to search these collections successfully is limited to those trained in the study of Christian iconography. Describing the primary subject matter of a medieval work of art from one of these collections, we identify "a male figure holding fruit" as one of many representational elements. But "male holding fruit" is a relatively general description. Does it symbolize St. Sabas, who is regularly depicted holding an apple, or the Fall of Man in which Adam is likely to be holding the infamous apple presented to him by Eve? To link these representational elements with their symbolic implication, we must have knowledge of biblical events and the history of the Christian church, knowledge that requires training in Christian iconography, art history, or medieval studies.

Primary subject matter can be used to develop a searching aid to collections of visual images (in this example, iconographical research collections) so that users who do not have knowledge and training in Christian iconography or related fields can search these collections. Such a searching aid links secondary subject matter with its corresponding primary subject matter. Consulting the searching aid, users can translate primary subject matter into secondary subject matter and then access the collection of visual images under the appropriate terminology (represented as secondary subject matter).

Panofsky (1962, 6) delineates the close relationship between primary and secondary subject matter in his definition of iconographical analysis:

That a male figure with a knife represents St. Bartholomew, that a female figure with a peach in her hand is a personification of veracity, ...we connect artistic motifs...with themes and concepts. Motifs thus recognized as carriers of a secondary or conventional meaning may be called images...stories, and allegories. The identification of such images, stories, and allegories is the domain of iconography.

One can ascribe secondary meaning to an image based on knowledge of its primary subject matter. As in Panofsky's example, the iconographer connects the elements of preiconographical description—objects, expressional qualities, and events (level 1)—with their respective themes and concepts (level 2). In Panofsky's example, the key to discovering secondary meaning is simply to identify correctly the elements of preiconographical description and match them with their counterparts in secondary subject matter.

A searching aid to collections of visual images to help searchers translate primary subject matter into secondary subject matter is not meant to replace one means of access with the other. Rather, the searching aid will help searchers, especially nonsubject specialists who are likely to approach a collection of visual images with knowledge of primary subject matter, and at the same time maintain the secondary subject matter approach for subject specialists who have thus far been the chief end users of collections of visual images. I call this searching aid a thematic catalog of primary and secondary subject matter. To compile such a catalog, a computer application called cluster analysis is used; consequently descriptions of the primary subject matter of visual images are entered into machine-readable form.

Such machine-readable descriptions, or data records, can be used for a number of purposes, the most obvious of which is to index the records in a computerized information storage and retrieval system for subject searching. To facilitate finding the image in the collection, empirical data about the actual image itself (such as title, photographer, artist, date, and filing location) would be added to these records. Table 1.2 is an adaptation of a table by Lindsay (1968) combining the three levels of interpretation identified by Panofsky and by Ackerman (1963) into a table to indicate the availability of data in each level to convert into machine-readable form. Ackerman added the empirical level to Panofsky's table to take into consideration information about a visual image such as physical details of height and width and historical details such as date of execution and artist. Lindsay's table indicates that empirical data and secondary subject matter are currently available for conversion into machine-readable form, but primary subject matter is not. Primary subject matter could improve data records for individual visual images by providing better subject access to help nonsubject specialists who lack knowledge of secondary subject matter query a database using primary subject matter and retrieve records to satisfy their request.

Data records with primary subject matter need not be constrained by size as are records created for manual files. The data records can be easily indexed in the computer in ways that have been prohibitively expensive using manual files.

Primary subject matter descriptions of visual images are the foundation for building a searching aid to collections of visual images so that these collections can be accessed by users who do not know the secondary subject matter of visual images. Chapter 2 presents a step-by-step approach to the process of compiling such a thematic catalog.

Table 1.2
Data Availability per Level of Interpretation for Conversion into Machine-readable Form

Levels of Interpretation		Is Data Available for Computer Input?
Panofsky	Ackerman	
1. Pre-iconographical description (or Primary Subject Matter) A. Factual B. Expressional C. Pseudo-formal	1. Empirical (for example, title, photographer, date executed, measurements, etc.)	Yes
	2. Analytic A. Formal Conventions B. Symbolic Conventions	No
2. Iconographical Analysis (or Secondary Subject Matter)	3. Intuitive (Synthetic)	Yes
3. Iconological Interpretation (or Intrinsic Meaning)		No (but probably not necessary)

SOURCE: Partially based on Kenneth C. Lindsay "Computer Input Form for Art Works," in Computers and Their Potential Applications in Museums (New York: Arno Press, 1968), p. 25.

2 A Step-by-Step Approach to Compiling a Thematic Catalog of Primary and Secondary Subject Matter

2.1 INTRODUCTION

Eight steps are needed to compile a thematic catalog of primary and secondary subject matter (fig. 2.1):

Step 1A: Visual images are selected.

Step 1B: Indexers are selected.

Step 2:   Indexers formulate preiconographical descriptions to artworks.

Step 3:   Composite descriptions are prepared.

Step 4:   Composite descriptions are compared using cluster analysis.

Step 5:   Clusters in context are created.

Step 6:   Iconographers are selected.

Step 7:   Iconographers interpret the secondary meaning of clusters in context.

Step 8:   The thematic catalog of primary and secondary subject matter is compiled.

I used these steps in an experiment to test the method of compiling a thematic catalog for works of art in an iconographical research collection. In practice, some steps may be unnecessary or may be altered should a catalog be compiled to support an existing collection of visual images.

Figure 2.1
Flowchart of the Process of Compiling a Thematic Catalog

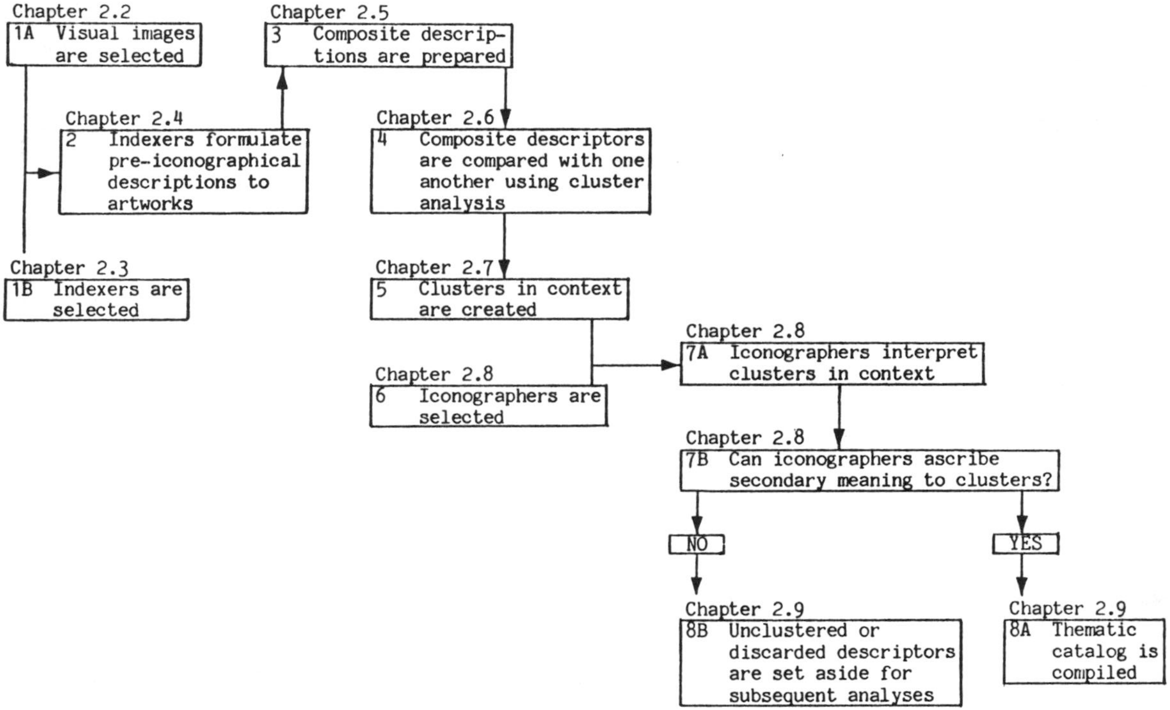

Chapter 2.2
1A Visual images are selected

Chapter 2.4
2 Indexers formulate pre-iconographical descriptions to artworks

Chapter 2.3
1B Indexers are selected

Chapter 2.5
3 Composite descriptions are prepared

Chapter 2.6
4 Composite descriptors are compared with one another using cluster analysis

Chapter 2.7
5 Clusters in context are created

Chapter 2.8
6 Iconographers are selected

Chapter 2.8
7A Iconographers interpret clusters in context

Chapter 2.8
7B Can iconographers ascribe secondary meaning to clusters?

NO

YES

Chapter 2.9
8A Thematic catalog is compiled

Chapter 2.9
8B Unclustered or discarded descriptors are set aside for subsequent analyses

2.2   VISUAL IMAGES ARE SELECTED

One hundred works of art executed in Northern Europe between 1250 and 1425 were selected for the experiment to test the method. This period in Western art was chosen because artists infused their works with a level of meaning that transcended the work's representational elements and penetrated to the depths of philosophical and religious thought. There was great certainty that the content depicted in these visual images exemplified primary subject matter and secondary meaning. Furthermore, the style of art at this time was primarily representational, so indexers with minimal training in observing and interpreting works of art would have little difficulty recognizing the elements of primary subject matter: objects, events, and expressional qualities. This is in keeping with Panofsky's corrective principle of interpretation, the history of style (see table 1.1), with which indexers must be familiar in order to identify correctly primary subject matter.

Colored 35 mm slide reproductions of panel paintings and manuscript illuminations from this period were selected from the art history slide collections of two upstate New York university libraries. Titles of 20 of the 100 works of art and their source are listed in appendix A. Other empirical data included in the appendix are artist (if known), date of execution, owning institution, and citations to reproductions in secondary sources. Identifying data, such as the date of execution and artist, were transcribed from the descriptive labels pasted on the 35 mm slides and verified in the secondary sources listed.

For the purpose of the experiment, a work of art was that portion of the total art object that was interpretable as a scene; that is, the content of the artwork was independent of the remainder of the artwork for interpretation. Details of artworks (portions or parts of a scene) were not selected. We did not have the problem of representing a three-dimensional object like sculpture or the decorative arts on a two-dimensional medium because reproductions of panel painting and manuscript illumination depict the entire entity rather than one of many viewpoints of the object.

In practice, this step of selecting visual images will probably be unnecessary because a thematic catalog of primary and secondary subject matter would normally be compiled to support the users and uses of an existing collection.

2.3 INDEXERS ARE SELECTED

Candidates for selection as indexers in this experiment were self-sufficient adults. The task of these individuals possessing an everyday commonsense knowledge of the world—identifying primary subject matter in works of art from iconographical research collections—presupposed practical experience, or "familiarity with objects and events" (Panofsky, 1955, 40–41):

The objects and events whose representation by lines, colours and volumes constitutes the world of *motifs* can be identified, as we have seen, on the basis of our practical experience. *Everybody* can recognize the shape and behaviour of human beings, animals and plants, and *everybody* can tell an angry face from a jovial one. (Panofsky, 1962, 9; italics added)

Panofsky thus asserts that everybody can elicit a description of subject matter. If the primary subject matter of iconographical research collections were described, then anyone—meaning everyone—could search iconographical research collections.

In the experiment, we sought individuals who had no or limited training in Christian iconography and related disciplines as a safeguard against obtaining descriptions of secondary subject matter. After they finished describing works of art, the volunteer indexers filled out a questionnaire that inquired into the nature and extent of their art background and any significant religious training that they felt helped them to describe the artworks. Responses of observers who reported instruction in applied art, art history, or religion were checked for secondary subject matter and sometimes omitted from the study.

The questionnaire also collected demographic information on observers. This information, summarized in chapter 3, provides a description of the educational and religious backgrounds of observers who successfully formulated preiconographical descriptions and reasons for the omission of the responses of some observers. The questionnaire is shown in figure 2.2.

Figure 2.2
Art Background Questionnaire

Please respond to the following questions.
All answers will be kept strictly confidential.

1. Sex:
   _____ Female
   _____ Male

2. Last grade attended:
   _____ High School
   _____ Vocational and Trade School
   _____ Junior College
   _____ Four-Year University or College
   _____ Graduate School
   _____ Other (Please specify: _____)

3. Major field of study in last grade attended: _____

4. Did you ever receive instruction in art, for example, drawing, painting, etc.?
   _____ Yes   _____ No
   If you answered No to question 4, skip to question 7.

5. In what types of teaching environments did you receive art instruction?
   (Check as many as needed:)
   _____ High School
   _____ Vocational and Trade School
   _____ Junior College
   _____ Four-Year University or College
   _____ Graduate School
   _____ Other (Please specify, for example, museum classes, camp, etc.: _____
   _____)

6. Describe the type of art instruction you received, for example, subject area of classes taken, how long, etc.
   _____
   _____
   _____

7. Did you ever receive instruction in the history of art?
   _____ Yes   _____ No
   If you answered No to questions, skip to question 10.

8. In what types of teaching environments did you receive instruction in the history of art?
   _____ High School
   _____ Vocational and Trade School
   _____ Junior College
   _____ Four-Year University or College
   _____ Graduate School
   _____ Other (Please specify: _____)

9. Describe the type of art history instruction you received. _____
   _____
   _____

10. Describe any important religious training or religious background which you have received that helped you to describe the artworks in this experiment.
    _____
    _____
    _____

THANK YOU FOR YOUR PARTICIPATION IN THIS EXPERIMENT.

2.4   INDEXERS FORMULATE PREICONOGRAPHICAL DESCRIPTIONS TO ARTWORKS

Indexers were given a packet containing three types of items in addition to the art background questionnaire: instructions, response forms, and works of art. They were instructed to view artworks one at a time and to formulate preiconographical descriptions for each work. Panofsky (1962, 5) delineated the composition of pre-iconographical description:

PRIMARY or NATURAL SUBJECT MATTER . . . is apprehended by identifying pure *forms*, that is: certain configurations of line and colour, or certain peculiarly shaped lumps of bronze or stone, as representations of natural *objects* such as human beings, animals, plants, houses, tools and so forth; by identifying their mutual relations as *events*; and by perceiving such *expressional* qualities as the mournful character of a pose or gesture, or the homelike and peaceful atmosphere of an interior. The world of pure *forms* thus recognized as carriers of *primary* or *natural meaning* may be called the world of artistic *motifs*. An enumeration of these motifs would be a *pre-iconographical* description of the work of art.

Much of Panofsky's definition of primary subject matter was adopted in this study but simplified when explained to indexers. The instructions given to indexers requested that they write down the subject matter present in works of art; primary subject matter was categorized into objects, expressional qualities, and events and defined for indexers as follows:

1. *Objects* name *things* and *people* in the artwork, for example, man, canopy, mountains.
2. *Expressional qualities* refer to *effects, feeling-states, sensations*, and *psychological nuances* conveyed by the objects in the artwork, for example, formidable, removed, enthusiastic.
3. *Events* relate the *actions* and *goings-on* in the artwork, for example, touching, pulling, inclined.

Figure 2.3 shows the response form indexers used to enumerate preiconographical descriptions.

Three indexers were used to formulate preiconographical description for each work of art. Thus, a single work of art was

Figure 2.3
Subject Matter Response Form

Please write down in the space below a description of
the subject matter in reproduction #_____, specifically its
objects, expressional qualities, and events.

OBJECTS	EXPRESSIONAL QUALITIES	EVENTS

described by three different indexers, and a composite of the responses was obtained later. Firschein and Fischler (1971a) employed this strategy to obtain completeness for the set of observers who viewed the same visual stimulus. More than one indexer formulated descriptions for each artwork in this study to attain completeness for the set of indexers with respect to the objects, expressional qualities, and events in works of art. Thirty-nine indexers formulated preiconographical descriptions to the 100 works of art in the experiment. In an actual work situation, only one indexer would be used to describe a single work of art, but volunteers were used in our experiment (and we could not expect them to describe all 100 artworks). Moreover, to discover the type of backgrounds that would affect indexers when identifying primary subject matter in works of art, we needed many indexers.

The instructions to indexers contained an example of an artwork and its preiconographical description on a completed response form to help them identify and describe primary subject matter. The description on the response form was a consensus of remarks obtained from five indexers whose backgrounds were similar to those of the volunteers in the study. The instructions to indexers are given in figure 2.4.

2.5   COMPOSITE PREICONOGRAPHICAL DESCRIPTIONS ARE PREPARED

Composite preiconographical descriptions were prepared in order to achieve normalization of nomenclature, consensus, and completeness for the set of three indexers who viewed the same artworks. These objectives were reported by Firschein and Fischler (1971a) when they offered a rationale for instituting this procedure into their study of untrained observers' responses to aerial photographs. To prepare these descriptions, we had to maintain records for preiconographical descriptors assigned by individual indexers and the artworks to which they were assigned and preiconographical descriptors constituting a composite description and the artwork to which they were assigned. These two items were in fact a single listing and acted as a cross-reference index and synonym dictionary so that prior use of preiconographical descriptors was easy to check in the course of preparing composite descriptions. At all times, as the composite describer, I was free to refer to this cross-reference and synonym dictionary or to the artworks themselves, particularly when one indexer had enumerated a preiconographical descriptor that the other two indexers had not. These unique descriptors were included in the composite preiconographical description only after the describer had inspected the work of art to ascertain whether the element was depicted and checked the cross-reference index to determine what form to prefer.

Figure 2.4
Instructions to Indexers

Subject Matter in Art Project

The purpose of this experiment is to use your responses and those of others to develop a special catalog to aid searchers of art pictures, photographs, and slides. Right now, I need to focus your attention on looking at reproductions of works of art and describing their subject matter. I will not be testing your ability to describe what you see in a work of art.

Enclosed are eight colored reproductions of works of art and eight blank forms for your responses. The reproductions and response forms are numbered to match. I would like you to examine each artwork and write down the subject matter, that is, the objects, events, and expressional qualities present in the artwork. Definitions of these three aspects are as follows:

1. Objects name things and people in the artwork, for example, man, canopy, mountains.

2. Expressional qualities refer to effects, feeling-states, sensations, and psychological nuances conveyed by the objects in the artwork, for example, formidable, removed, enthusiastic.

3. Events relate the actions and goings-on in the artwork, for example, touching, pulling, inclined.

An artwork reproduction and completed response form are given as examples on the following two pages. Examine this example carefully and think a few moments about what you would write down to describe its subject matter. Then read the description of objects, expressional qualities, and events following the artwork. If you do not agree with that description, note your changes on the response form on the example page.

Figure 2.4 (continued)

Passionsaltar, Kreuzannagelung, by Meister Bertram. By permission of the Niedersächsisches Landesmuseum Hannover.

Please write down in the space below a description of
the subject matter in reproduction #A, specifically its
objects, expressional qualities, and events.

OBJECTS	EXPRESSIONAL QUALITIES	EVENTS
Christ	Unaffected, removed	Being crucified, lying on cross, bearded, long-haired, dressed in loincloth
Crossed feet and outstretched hands		Bound with rope, pierced with spikes, spurting blood
Ornate halo and crown of thorns		
Cross		Sturdy, wooden, lying on hill, rough-hewn
3 Workmen	Intent, concentrating	Tightening rope, wearing stocking cap, lying on ground
1 Woman	Intent	Tightening rope, wearing stocking cap, lying on ground
1 Workman	Pleased, enthusiastic, enjoying	Hammering spike, balding
Jagged Rocks	Dark, formidable	
3-Stemmed Flowers		
Anthills		

The foregoing example is meant to acquaint you with the task of describing
the subject matter of works of art. Note that the expressional qualities and
events associated with specific objects are listed together in the same row.
Soemtimes objects do not portray expressional qualities or do not depict
events, for example, "crown of thorns." In other instances, objects cannot be
separated from events, for example, "dressed in loincloth." Try to format your
response as best as you can into the appropriate columns of the response form.

Four points to remember:

1. Examine the work of art carefully and write down as many objects,
   events, and expressional qualities as you can.

2. You may find that some artworks do not contain any events or
   expressional qualities.

3. It is important that you do not compare one reproduction to another.
   Describe each one separately.

4. Limit yourself to 15 minutes when describing a work of art.

When you are finished describing the reproductions, complete the Art
Background Questionnaire. Then return all materials, that is, reproductions,
response forms, and questionnaire, to the pockets of the folder.

Thank you for your participation in this project!

23

Figure 2.5 sets forth six guidelines for preparing composite preiconographical descriptions; by following these guidelines, such descriptions can be prepared from the primary subject matter descriptions of a single visual image. In practice, however, there would normally only be one indexer per visual image, so the preparation and composite descriptions would be unnecessary. Composite descriptions to 20 of the 100 works of art used to compile the thematic catalog in this study are given in appendix A.

2.6   COMPOSITE PREICONOGRAPHICAL DESCRIPTIONS ARE COMPARED USING CLUSTER ANALYSIS

The clustering procedure incorporated into the process of compiling a thematic catalog of primary and secondary subject matter, developed by Gerard Salton and Anita Wong, was obtained from the Department of Computer Science at Cornell University. Salton and Wong (1978) relied on the earlier work of Rocchio (1966) and Williamson (1974) to develop the clustering technique. They describe the technique used in this study as single-pass clustering, which proceeds bottom-up and generates a tree structure as an end product. Automatic classification of items is complete after a single pass through the entire file of items. As items are added to the existing tree structure, the tree is rearranged. The cost of searching the existing tree to find nodes with which incoming items share a sufficient degree of similarity is proportional to the log of the number of items contained in the existing tree.

The process of generating clusters employs the single-pass method. It has two major operations: (1) searching existing clusters to find one (or more) whose similarity (cosine) coefficient with an incoming item is sufficiently large and, if necessary, (2) splitting existing clusters whose size exceeds a predetermined level.

In applying the clustering procedure, preiconographical descriptors assigned to an artwork were compared to all other preiconographical descriptors and the artworks to which they were assigned. In short, the outcome of the clustering procedure was clusters of preiconographical descriptors.

Figure 2.5
Guidelines for Preparing Composite Descriptions

1. Familiarize Yourself with the Descriptions

   First, become familiar with observers' descriptions by reading each one and taking time to match objects with one another. Usually the first three or four objects listed on each form match with those on the other forms.

2. Find Consensus Terms

   Write down objects, expressional qualities, and events that match among all three responses or between two of three responses. In order to determine matched terms, find those words that:

   a. match exactly letter-for-letter, e.g., sitting = sitting, ornate throne = ornate throne

   b. are the same but differ with respect to single and multiple words, e.g., bare foot = barefoot, or loincloth = loin cloth

   c. are the same but differ with respect to their endings (except for singular and plural forms which must be counted as different terms), e.g., sitting = seated, or carry = carried (but cushion ≠ cushions, so list each separately)

   d. are the same but differ with respect to punctuation, e.g., Christ's face = face of Christ

   e. are abbreviations, e.g., st. = saint, or saints = ss.

   f. are synonyms, e.g., quiet = silent, or pillows = cushions. Check a dictionary, Roget's thesaurus, etc., if in doubt

3. Find Unique Terms

   Write down those objects, expressional qualities, and events that only one observer has listed and terms that are not comparable among those listed by the other two observers. If in doubt whether the element is depicted, view the artwork in question.

4. What to do with Discrepancies among Terms

   In a number of instances, one of three responses (or two of three, or one of two, or all three responses) will be neither synonyms nor word variants due to spelling, abbreviations, etc. The following are suggestions concerning what response to select.

   a. Prefer the majority, i.e., two of three

   b. View the artwork itself and figure out how you would have described the element in question

   c. Check the descriptor and cross-reference index to find out what other artworks are assigned the term and the way in which that term is represented in the artwork(s) as an object, expressional quality, or event

Figure 2.5 (continued)

    d. If the term in question names a person, prefer the most general form, e.g., choose "man" from the terms "Peter," "Saint," "man"

5. Remember Special Exceptions

When writing down objects, expressional qualities, and events, remember the following special exceptions:

    a. Prefer English to foreign terms, e.g., prefer dead to morte

    b. Prefer active voice to passive voice, especially when designating events, e.g., prefer "stable covers" to "is covered by"

    c. Do not identify objects, expressional qualities, or events more than once in a single description, e.g., praying and kneeling, or town and castle, houses, windows, shutters, etc.

    d. Omit affective type responses, e.g., "throne-like," "beautiful painting," etc.

    e. Omit formalist type responses, e.g., "two-dimensional rendering," "oblong-shaped projection," etc.

    f. Omit location type responses, e.g., "between them," "toward," or "on the right," etc.

    g. Omit guesses, e.g., "looks like a church," or "man?"

6. Prepare the Composite Description

Once you have selected all consensus and unique terms, integrate all terms into an English language paragraph format. For example, the following terms were selected as pre-iconographical descriptors to a Crucifixion scene:

haloed	mouth	cross-(1)	dying	opened
bleeding	Mary	supporting	clenched	spikes
head	sad	skullcap	dressed	thoughtful
plaque	blue-gown	man-(1)	feet	hands-(2)
Christ	green-gown	hand-(1)	nailed	suffering

Organized in a list fashion, these terms make no apparent sense to the reader. However, placed into the context of a paragraph, the terms provide the reader with a mental image of the scene:

    Haloed Christ, wearing skullcap, dying on cross-(1), mouth opened, suffering, nailed, bleeding from clenched hands-(2) and feet at spikes. Plaque on cross-(1). Mary dressed in blue-gown, sad, thoughtful. Sad man-(1) dressed in green-gown, supporting his head with hand-(1).

The clustering procedure uses the comparison of preiconographical descriptors as an example. The procedure is controlled by parameters such as the amount of overlap between clusters (MAXCOV), and the minimum (MINSPLIT) and maximum (MAXSPLIT or DIVIDE) size of clusters. All of these parameters can be set by the researcher; others are set by the clustering procedure at default values.

Record 1, a preiconographical descriptor and the artwork numbers to which it is assigned, is input into the clustering environment. Since record 1 is the first item allowed into the clustering environment, nothing is available for comparison; thus record 1 becomes the first cluster, $A[1]$. A special identification tag called a centroid vector is constructed to represent $A[1]$. The centroid vector, C, is the total number of unique descriptors, d, for every member of $A[1]$, or

$$C = \Sigma d^{(i)}$$
$$d^{(i)} \epsilon A_{[1]}.$$

Record 2, another preiconographical descriptor and the artwork numbers to which it is assigned, is entered into the clustering environment and joins the existing cluster, $A[1]$. The centroid vector, C, is redefined to include the descriptors unique to both members of the cluster. More records are input and join $A[1]$ until $A[1]$ equals MINSPLIT, a parameter that controls the minimum number of members allowed in a cluster before splitting is allowed. If attempts to split the cluster fail, more records are input and join $A[1]$ until $A[1]$ equals MAXSPLIT, a parameter that controls the maximum number of members allowed in the first cluster before splitting must occur.

Cluster splitting begins with the construction of an $a \times a$ similarity matrix of pairwise correlation coefficients (where a = number of members in the cluster marked for splitting). Trial clusters exhibiting the greatest amount of overlap with other trial clusters are selected to replace the existing cluster; centroids are constructed from the members of the newly generated clusters. Some members of the old cluster may not be sufficiently similar to the newly generated clusters, dubbed "loose" members by Salton and Wong (1978). These loose members are either inserted into the most similar newly generated cluster or allowed to form a new cluster.

When cluster splitting is complete, another record enters into the clustering environment. The incoming record is compared with existing cluster centroids and added to the most similar cluster based on an analysis of the similarity coefficient of the incoming records and the similarity coefficient of existing clusters. When the record joins a cluster, the cluster centroid of this cluster is redefined to include the newly admitted member of the cluster. If the number of members contained in that cluster equals the number specified by the parameter DIVIDE, the cluster splitting process becomes operational.

Cluster generation and splitting continue until there are no more records to enter into the clustering environment. The output of the clustering procedure is a tree structure; the nodes of the tree structure are the structure's vertices, and the leaves of the structure are preiconographical descriptors. A portion of a tree structure generated from clustering of preiconographical descriptors is shown in figure 2.6.

Figure 2.6
Tree Structure Resulting from Clustering Preiconographical Descriptors

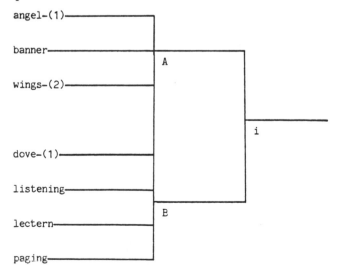

Overlapping cluster analysis was used in this study to group elements of primary subject matter because it is logical, given the nature of primary subject matter in medieval art, that an element could be distributed into more than one cluster. For example, a cluster of preiconographical descriptors relating to the theme "Christ Bearing the Cross" and a cluster of preiconographical descriptors relating to the theme "Christ Crucified" are very likely to contain the preiconographical descriptor *cross*, since the cross plays a major role in both themes.

This clustering procedure has some important shortcomings. First, it was part of a larger computer program whose overall purpose was information retrieval. The routine was constructed with no idea that the composition of individual clusters would ever be manually inspected or interpreted. Thus the practice of splitting clusters when they exceeded a certain size may help to minimize searching costs in information retrieval, but it has the potential of creating unnatural boundaries between clusters. This problem is somewhat mitigated by the fact that a cluster that has been forced to split into two shares the same parent as its brother, so both brothers might be interpreted as a single cluster.

The problem of clustering loose (miscellaneous) items in an information retrieval environment is perplexing; in fact, Salton and Wong (1978, 327) remarked that "efficient solution appears to be lacking." They treat this problem in their clustering procedure by implementing either of two practices: loose items are merged with similar existing clusters, or a cluster of loose items is constructed. Both practices may be considered adequate in an information retrieval environment where every document in the collection must be accessible for retrieval.

In this study, the second practice, constructing a cluster of loose items, is preferred. Ideally loose items ought to remain unclustered, but the Salton-Wong procedure lacks this option. The two practices used to cluster loose items are dubious ones because the procedure gives no feedback about the identity of loose items merged with existing clusters or clusters constructed of loose items—an important drawback of the clustering procedure used in this study. Acknowledging that some clusters or members of well-formed clusters bear a miscellaneous quality may be the only course of action short of reprogramming the clustering package. These drawbacks, however, emphasize important features for constructing an optimum clustering procedure to be used in developing a thematic catalog.

The routine is also order dependent, a flaw that might be overcome by submitting data two or more times in a different order and comparing the output. Of course, the object of this study is not to achieve stable clusters but meaningful ones (that is, clusters whose composition can be ascribed secondary meaning by iconographical experts).

In the process of preparing composite preiconographical descriptions, every work of art was described preiconographically, as in this example:

3060 woman-(1), 2021 silent and 1002 haloed, 1005 dressed in 3064 cape, 1006 holding in 3055 hands-(2) 3061 cloth with 3062 Christ's face, which is 2023 morose and with 2024 longing in his 3063 dark eyes, and 3058 long hair, 1014 bearded and haloed.

Four-digit numbers were assigned to every unique preiconographical descriptor, such as *woman-(1)*, *silent*, and so on, because the clustering program would only accept numbers as the raw data. One limit of the clustering procedure used in this study was that the output of the clustering routine was a list of four-digit numbers that had to be transformed into their English-language equivalents. We learned to compensate for this limit given the advantages of the clustering procedure on the whole.

The clustering procedure used in this study was developed at Cornell University for experiments in information retrieval and document representations. Cluster analysis procedures have been thoroughly described and evaluated in review articles (Cormack, 1971; Williams, 1971) and textbooks (Jardine and Sibson, 1971; Sneath and Sokal, 1973; Clifford and Stephenson, 1975; Hartigan, 1975; Salton, 1975). University computer centers and facilities often support cluster analysis programs or statistical analysis packages that feature cluster analysis programs. Frequently the cluster analysis programs supported are hierarchical and nonoverlapping. Overlapping programs that have been used for research and experimental purposes are sometimes available for the asking. These programs require mainframe computers; to our knowledge, cluster analysis has not yet been done on minicomputers or microcomputers.

2.7 CLUSTERS IN CONTEXT ARE CREATED

Step 5, creating clusters in context, pertains to computer-generated groups of preiconographical descriptors. The output of the clustering procedure is a list of automatically generated groups of preiconographical descriptors. Since overlapping cluster analysis was used, a preiconographical descriptor could be assigned to more than one automatically generated group. In practice, the output resembled the tree structure of figure 2.7, in which preiconographical descriptors constituted the leaves of the tree.

We conceived the idea of creating clusters in context as a means of presenting cluster composition to iconographers. Comparable automatic classification and thesaurus experiments in the past have proved inconclusive. For example, nuclear physicists were asked to interpret a factor-analytically derived automatic classification (Atherton and Borko, 1965, 7). When they interpreted eight groups of automatically derived terms, "they compared this work effort to the game of making a story around five words chosen at random."

Consider how to interpret the cluster of preiconographical descriptors in figure 2.6. We did not want iconographers to describe the task of naming clustered preiconographical descriptors as a game, so we sought a way of reinstating clustered preiconographical descriptors into the context of the preiconographical description in which they occurred. The result was an activity to create clusters in context. Iconographers were given clusters in context to interpret rather than the raw output of the computer, a list of clustered preiconographical descriptors.

The tree structure generated by the clustering procedure comprises many levels. Figure 2.7 is an example of a hypothetical tree structure resulting from a cluster analysis. The tree has three levels and seventeen vertices; the lowest level of the tree corresponds to the preiconographical descriptors themselves. When

Figure 2.7
Hypothetical Tree Structure Resulting from a Cluster Analysis of 66
Preiconographical Descriptors

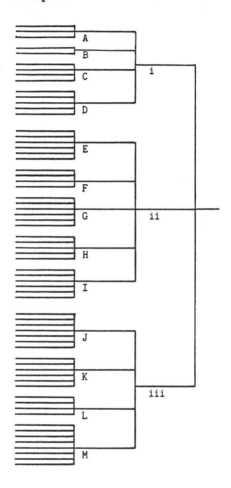

NOTE: Letters refer to <u>lowest level vertices</u>. Lower case Roman numerals refer
to <u>second lowest level vertices</u>.

forming clusters in context, the two lowest levels are examined. In the example in figure 2.7, clusters in context are created from the thirteen lowest-level clusters and three second-level clusters.

Vertex E contains six preiconographical descriptors: *gentle, praising, observant, removed, joyous,* and *curious.* The following list shows which artworks (by number) contained these descriptors:

Descriptor	Artwork Numbers
Gentle	60 89 92
Praising	5 92 99
Observant	1 8 17 20 30 45 47 49 50 52 73 75 76 78 79 90 92 95
Removed	5 6 9 27 32 33 38 39 49 58 60 71 76 77 82 87 90 98
Joyous	5 23 83 92 93 100
Curious	15 60 83 94 98 99 100

The artwork number signifies that the preiconographical descriptor is used at least once for that artwork. Calculating frequencies of artwork numbers, one finds that the preiconographical descriptions of artwork numbers 5, 60, and 92 contain at least half of the six preiconographical descriptors listed. The following list shows preiconographical descriptors accompanied by the context in which they are found in the descriptions of artwork numbers 5, 60, and 92:

1. No. 60: One of girls-(2) standing, reaching, *gentle*
   No. 92: Angel-(1) praising, *gentle*
2. No. 5: Angel-(1) *praising*, with arms-(2) outstretched
   No. 92: Angel-(1) *praising*, kneeling, and offering
4. No. 5: Mary, *removed*, sitting on ornate throne
   No. 60: Animals, *removed*, feeding
5. No. 5: Angels-(2) *joyous* with arms-(2) outstretched
   No. 92: Angel-(1) *joyous*, praising

When preiconographical descriptors are reinstated into the context of the preiconographical description, only the second of five descriptors, *praising*, is used in a similar fashion in the context of the description. In this example, a cluster in context cannot be created because more than one preiconographical descriptor used in a similar context as another descriptor is needed to form a group or cluster in context.

Vertex H contains the following preiconographical descriptors:

Descriptor	Artwork Numbers
Praising	5 92 99
Lap	5 9 19 43 66 75 82 87 100
Kings-(3)	43 66 73 94
Gifts	43 66 73 94
Offering	43 48 55 65 66 73 80 82 92 94

Calculating frequencies of artwork numbers, one finds that the preiconographical descriptions of artwork numbers 43, 66, 73, and 94 contain at least half of the five descriptors. The preiconographical descriptors are listed below, accompanied by the context in which they are found in the preiconographical description:

2. No. 43: Mary holding in her *lap* Infant Christ
    No. 66: Mary holding in her arm-(1) and *lap* Infant Christ
3. No. 43: *Kings-(3)* with crown
    No. 66: *Kings-(3)* with crown
    No. 73: *Kings-(3)* with crown
    No. 94: *Kings-(3)* with crown
4. No. 43: Kings-(3) offering *gifts*
    No. 66: Kings-(3) offering *gifts*
    No. 73: Kings-(3) offering *gifts*
    No. 94: Kings-(3) offering *gifts*
5. No. 43: Kings-(3) *offering* gifts
    No. 66: Kings-(3) *offering* gifts
    No. 73: Kings-(3) *offering* gifts
    No. 94: Kings-(3) *offering* gifts

Examining these preiconographical descriptors as they occur in the context of the preiconographical description reveals similarities in their use, particularly the descriptors *Kings-(3) with crown* and *Kings-(3) offering gifts*. The preiconographical descriptor *lap* is used in a similar but not exact manner in the preiconographical descriptions of artworks 43 and 66. *Lap* is included in the descriptive phrases as part of the basic concept of "Mary Holding the Infant Christ." The descriptive phrase of artwork 66 in which the Infant is held in Mary's arm and lap serves as an amplification of the descriptive phrase of artwork 43. Thus, all four descriptive phrases were used to construct the cluster in context. Remember that iconographers examine clusters in context and interpret their meaning. If there is any question concerning the similarity between descriptive phrases, we include the descriptive phrases in question. Thus the iconographers are the final judges of cluster composition.

Clusters in context are formatted by alphabetizing clustered preiconographical descriptors and rearranging the descriptive phrases in a keyword in context fashion. Thus the four phrases constituting the second example, as formulated into a cluster in context, are:

Kings-(3) offering gifts

Kings-(3) with crown

Mary holding Infant Christ in her lap

Mary holding Infant Christ in her arm-(1) and lap

Detailed guidelines for creating clusters in context are given in figure 2.8.

2.8   ICONOGRAPHERS INTERPRET SECONDARY MEANING OF CLUSTERS IN CONTEXT

If preiconographical elements cluster together because they are related with respect to secondary meaning, a thematic catalog of primary and secondary subject matter can be developed.

Secondary subject matter cannot be defined without being allied to primary subject matter (Panofsky, 1962, 6):

SECONDARY or CONVENTIONAL SUBJECT MATTER . . . is apprehended by realizing . . . that a female figure with a peach in her hand

Figure 2.8
Guidelines for Creating Clusters in Context

1. List the pre-iconographical descriptors and the artwork numbers in which
   they occur. These pre-iconographical descriptors may be clustered in the
   lowest level of the tree structure or second lowest level of the tree. For
   example, the following five pre-iconographical descriptors were clustered
   in the lowest level of a tree:

   a. Loving
      Artwork nos.: 6 13 19 34 53 54 60 63 69 71 72 75 83

   b. Silent
      Artwork nos.: 6 7 13 18 20 60 71 73 97

   c. Grieving
      Artwork nos.: 2 6 13 48 50 55 69 70 93

   d. Men-(2)
      Artwork nos.: 6 13 36 37 42 48 58 68 74 80 100

   e. Open-casket
      Artwork nos.: 2 6 12 13

2. Single out those artworks whose pre-iconographical descriptions contain at
   least more than half of the clustered pre-iconographical descriptors. In
   the example above, artwork nos. 6 and 13 are common to more than half of
   the five descriptors.

3. When a pre-iconographical descriptor occurs in at least two
   pre-iconographical descriptions, find the pre-iconographical descriptor in
   the original description and compare its use in the context of other
   pre-iconographical descriptions in which it occurs. For example, all five
   pre-iconographical descriptors listed above occur in the pre-iconographical
   descriptions of at least two artworks--in this case artworks 6 and 13.

   Pre-iconographical descriptions of artworks 6 and 13 are given below. The
   five pre-iconographical descriptors co-occurring in these descriptions are
   underlined.

   Artwork 6
   Christ, haloed, long-hair, removed, wrapped in sheer-cloth, dressed in
   loincloth, and lying on open-casket. Feet and hands-(2) bleeding as
   men-(2), loving, both bearded and long-hair and one with cap, are
   placing him in smooth-casket. Women-(2), man-(1) with curly-hair, and
   Mary, all haloed, standing, silent and grieving. Stony-ground.

   Artwork 13
   Christ, suffering and dead, haloed and dressed in loincloth, crown of
   thorns, and wrapped in sheer-cloth, hands-(2) bleeding with gash in
   chest, lying on open-casket. Mary grieving and compassionate,
   touching hand-(1), women-(2), haloed standing, loving and caring.
   Men-(2), sad and bearded, placing Christ in casket. Man-(1) with
   crown, standing and silent, holding container and spoon. Onlookers.

It is easy to compare the use of descriptors in the context of the
pre-iconographical description when descriptive phrases in which the
pre-iconographical descriptors occur are listed side-by-side.

  6 Men-(2) placing Christ in smooth-casket
13 Men-(2) placing Christ in casket

  6 Men-(2), loving, placing Christ in smooth-casket
13 Women-(2), loving and caring, haloed, standing

  6 Women-(2) and Mary, all standing, silent
13 Man-(1) standing, silent, holding container

  6 Women-(2), man-(1), and Mary, all standing, grieving
13 Mary, grieving, touching hand-(1)

  6 Christ lying on open-casket
13 Christ lying on open-casket

Examining the first four descriptive phrases above one notes that only the
pre-iconographical descriptor "Men-(2)" is used in context similarly. This
single pre-iconographical descriptor does not constitute a cluster in
context, as more than one pre-iconographical descriptor is needed to create
a cluster in context.

Note: Instead of discarding all the pre-iconographical descriptors
above, consider forming clusters in context from the second
lowest level of the tree structure. In this way, the
pre-iconographical descriptor "Men-(2)" is not lost but merged
with a larger pool of pre-iconographical descriptors. Steps 1,
2, and 3 are then repeated for the larger pool of descriptors.

4. When pre-iconographical descriptors are placed in context, to create
clusters in context, select those descriptive phrases that duplicate one
another. In the example above, descriptive phrases containing "Men-(2)"
vary. The phrase "Men-(2) placing Christ in smooth-casket" reveals a
tactile quality, i.e., smoothness of the casket, which is not revealed in
the other phrase. Since this term merely introduces additional information
about one of the representational elements, it does not alter the overall
import of the phrase. Include descriptive phrases that serve to amplify
other phrases or are more specific than other phrases.

If there is any question about including a descriptive phrase, remember
that iconographers will be reviewing clusters in context and determining
the meaning of clustered pre-iconographical phrases. So include the phrase
and let the iconographer be the final judge.

5. Having selected descriptive phrases for the cluster in context, format them
alphabetically by clustered pre-iconographical descriptors and organize
them in a keyword in context format. For example, the descriptive phrases
above chosen for inclusion in a cluster in context are organized as:

                      Men-(2) placing Christ in casket
                      Men-(2) placing Christ in smooth-casket
        Christ lying on open-casket

is a personification of veracity, or that a group of figures in a certain arrangement and in certain poses represents the Last Supper.... In doing this we connect artistic motifs ... with *themes* and *concepts*. Motifs thus recognized as carriers of a *secondary or conventional meaning* may be called images ... stories and allegories. The identification of such images, stories and allegories is the domain of ... iconography. (Italics added)

Panofsky's definition of secondary meaning gives examples of some representational elements in artworks; for example, "female with a peach in her hand" indicates the concept of veracity, and "figures in a certain arrangement and in certain poses" indicates the theme of the Last Supper. Unlike primary subject matter, secondary subject matter is not the interpretation of concrete forms as bearers of meaning; rather, it is abstracted from the forms themselves and comprehensible only to those who know the literary themes and concepts from which it derives.

In this study, individuals capable of ascribing secondary meaning to preiconographical description are iconographical specialists. They know literary themes and concepts—a prerequisite for carrying out an iconographical analysis (see table 1.1).

In step 6, three iconographers are selected. In step 7, they are given clusters in context formulated in step 5 and asked to ascribe secondary meaning to these clusters. The raw data used to formulate clusters in context were obtained from cluster analyses of preiconographical descriptors.

Each iconographer received a folder containing instructions (figure 2.9) and clusters in context (figure 2.10). The iconographers were instructed to examine clusters in context one at a time and name the theme that the cluster in context expressed. They were asked to report any difficulties they encountered naming the theme.

2.9 THEMATIC CATALOG OF PRIMARY AND SECONDARY SUBJECT MATTER IS COMPILED

A thematic catalog of primary and secondary subject matter can be compiled if iconographical specialists determine that clustered preiconographical descriptors refer to secondary meaning. Primary subject matter is linked with its corresponding themes

Figure 2.9
Instructions to Iconographers

Subject Matter in Art Project

The purpose of this exercise is to link phrases describing the representational elements shared by a group of works of art to their general theme. Your participation will help us evaluate a computer-generated catalog to themes and concepts in artworks.

On the following pages are listed descriptive phrases denoting the representational elements, i.e., objects, events, and expressional qualities, shared by a group of artworks. The computer has grouped together the underlined words in every phrase.

Your task is to read the descriptive phrases listed on a page and see if a theme can be named that the group expresses.

Some points to remember:

1. Read each page and name the theme in the order given. Please do not read page 4 before page 3, etc.

2. Read each page and name the theme without referring to any pages preceding or following.

3. If a theme cannot be named, briefly describe your difficulty and then proceed to the next page. Please do not turn back to the page at a later time.

Many thanks for your participation in this project.

and concepts by iconographical specialists when they interpret clusters in context in step 7 of the process of compiling a thematic catalog.

The thematic catalog contains alphabetical listings of themes and concepts and their essential attributes, much the same as listings in iconographical dictionaries and indexes (Bailey and Pool, 1925; Ferguson, 1967; Sill, 1975). Individual objects, events, and expressional qualities are enumerated in a keyword-in-context format with cross-references to their equivalent secondary meaning.

An example that might be likened to the proposed thematic catalog is an alphabetical list of saints' emblems (Drake and Drake, 1916, 142, 180). Emblems (or primary subject matter), such as "anvil," "appearing," and "gridiron," are listed along with other emblems with which "anvil," "appearing," and "gridiron"

Figure 2.10
Two Examples of Clusters in Context on Worksheets Submitted to Iconographers

```
                           angel-(1) with wings-(2) kneeling before Mary
                           angel-(1) with wings-(2) stepping towards Mary
              angel-(1) holding banner
                           dove-(1) flying into Mary
                           dove-(1) flying into woman-(1)
Mary touching her chest with hand-(1)
                           Mary kneeling at lectern
                           Mary sitting on ornate throne
                           Mary sitting on throne
                           Mary standing at lectern
```

```
Name the theme described: _____
_____

If a theme cannot be named, briefly describe your difficulty: _____
_____
_____
_____
```

                        * * * * * * * * * * * * * * *

```
men-(3) with arms-(2) folded on knees
   Christ kneeling and praying on hill
              men-(3) sleeping and sitting on jagged ground
              men-(3) sleeping, crouching in grass
              trees and hills
              trees, jagged ground and hill
```

```
Name the theme described: _____
_____

If a theme cannot be named, briefly describe your difficulty: _____
_____
_____
_____
```

are likely to co-occur and the saints' names (or secondary subject matter) associated with those emblems:

Emblem	Co-occurring Emblem	Saint's Name
Anvil	armour, hammer and sword	Adrian
	crown and hammer on it	Eligius
	and forge near him	Apelles
	with severed hand on it	Adrian

Appearing	angel appearing to him	Fursey
	celestial palace appearing to him	Deusdedit
	cross appearing to him	Ephysius
	cross appearing to him	Geminian
	Our saviour, as a poor child	Peter
	Our saviour, in prison	Theodore
	world in flames appearing to him	Gabinus
Gridiron	and sword, in his hands	Laurence
	and sword, in his hands	Dionysius
	and sword, in his hands	Cyprian
	his bowels on a gridiron	Erasmus
	burnt on a gridiron	Donatella
	burnt on a gridiron	Eustratius
	burnt on a gridiron	Laurence
	burnt on a gridiron, and bowels torn with hook	Vincent
	as deacon, holding a gridiron	Laurence

In this example, saints' emblems might be likened to the descriptive phrases in clusters in context and saints' names to the general theme that the cluster in context expresses or to its secondary meaning. The task of iconographers is to determine the link between clusters in context and their general theme. The construction of the thematic catalog in step 8 is merely an exercise in rearranging the descriptive phrases of clusters in context and the general theme assigned by iconographers in step 7 of compiling a thematic catalog of primary and secondary subject matter so that the thematic catalog allows direct access to both primary and secondary subject matter.

The thematic catalog is a tool to aid end users of iconographical research collections who only have knowledge of primary subject matter (level-1-type information) to translate primary subject matter into the appropriate iconographical subject heading or descriptor and search the iconographical index or dictionary at hand. This catalog brings together a list of themes and concepts—secondary subject matter—and their essential attributes, expressed as objects, expressional qualities, and events.

3 Results of Compiling a Thematic Catalog of Primary and Secondary Subject Matter

3.1 INTRODUCTION

The process for compiling a thematic catalog is presented in flowchart format in figure 3.1. When this process was applied to works of art executed in Northern Europe from 1250 to 1425, the result was a thematic catalog of primary and secondary subject matter to these selected works of art.

3.2 INDEXERS' PRECONOGRAPHICAL DESCRIPTIONS

For this study, 100 works of art were selected. Indexers with a minimum art background and religious training were sought for the study. Each indexer was given a packet of materials containing instructions, response forms, reproductions of eight works of art, and an art background questionnaire. They were instructed to view the artworks one at a time and to write down the artworks' primary subject matter. Primary subject matter was categorized into objects, expressional qualities, and events.

We analyzed untrained indexers' descriptions of medieval works of art to find out how they responded to the task and, especially, the extent to which their descriptions deviated from primary subject matter and included formal properties, secondary subject matter, and other descriptive elements of works of art. Our examination should point out to others what types of

Figure 3.1
Flowchart of the Process of Compiling a Thematic Catalog

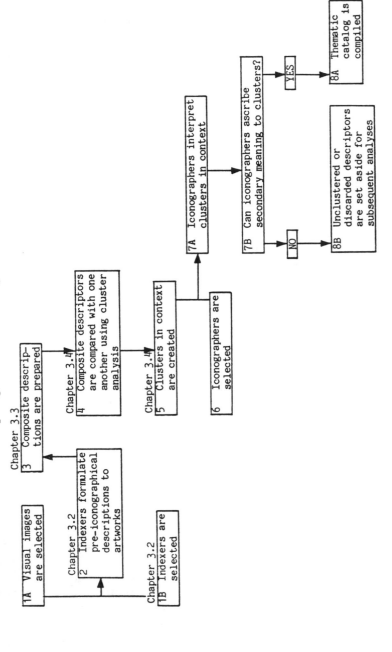

responses about medieval works of art are elicited from indexers who have no formal art history training to prepare them for the task of compiling a thematic catalog.

3.2.1 Indexers' Descriptions of Works of Art

Most experiments, such as those by experimental aestheticians Berlyne and Ogilvie (1974) or those employing the semantic differential (Osgood, Suci, and Tannenbaum, 1967; Canter, 1969), have placed restraints on observers. Typically such classification studies have not enlisted adjective qualifiers or unipolar categories drawn from respondents' actual responses. The results of these studies show only how observers responded to criteria designated by the researchers.

How do indexers without specialized training in art history talk and write about works of art when they are free from the restraints of rules or guiding principles? Cameron (1969), Firschein and Fischler (1971a), and Acuff and Sieber-Suppes (1972) placed no restraints on untrained observers and sought their unbridled responses to visual images. In an experiment described by Cameron, a sample of the Toronto public was interviewed about preferences in modern art. Cameron's study is important in the context of the present work because it demonstrated that individuals untrained in art have a predilection for identifying subject matter in works of art. Cameron (1969, 147) found that "people find it difficult to see beyond the subject matter, and when there is no recognizable subject matter, they are generally lost . . . they want to play the game of identification, not recognition." The implication is that untrained subjects are inclined to identify primary subject matter, as opposed to formal elements, when questioned about common elements in a group of works of art.

Acuff and Sieber-Suppes developed a content analysis manual and coding scheme to measure respondents' knowledge of works of art and classed respondents' statements about works of art into content analysis categories. We used their content analysis coding scheme to categorize the elements in the preiconographical descriptions of indexers whose descriptions were used in our study.

3.2.2 Indexers' Background

Forty-one indexers formulated primary subject matter descriptions to works of art in the process of compiling a thematic catalog (table 3.1). Ten, or approximately 25 percent, were males. Approximately 60 percent were between 20 and 29 years old; approximately 32 percent were between 30 and 39 years old. Only 7 percent were 40 years old or older.

The indexers were well educated. Forty had attended some educational institution after high school; over 80 percent had attended a four-year university or college or graduate school. Responses to the question about major field of study in last grade attended were categorized into 21 topic areas. The variety of responses demonstrates the wide range of academic backgrounds represented by the indexers. The two museum educators were involved with education in an upstate New York museum dealing with technological history and industrial archaeology. None of the occupations or fields of study reported related directly to the task of viewing and describing works of art.

3.2.3 Indexers' Art Background

Fifteen indexers (36 percent) reported having had instruction in applied art. Four had taken a studio course in art or a general media course at a four-year university or college; one had taken mechanical drawing in college. One indexer had been taught drawing and painting during her high school years by a private art instructor. Camp experience in sculpture and ceramics was reported by an indexer whose mother was an art teacher. Another indexer took drawing and painting classes at a local art guild and occasionally painted as a hobby. The indexer who graduated from a six-year university program in industrial design did not highlight any applied art courses relevant to the task of describing works of art. Thus the training in applied art received by indexers in this study did not seem particularly extensive; however, indexers who have had applied art training might refer to formal properties of works of art when formulating primary subject matter descriptions of works of art.

Table 3.1

Tallies of Answers from Art Background Questionnaire

41 Total number of observers	
31 Female observers	39 White observers
10 Male observers	2 Black observers

Last grade attended:

  1 High School
  2 Vocational and Technical School
  3 Junior College
  2 Nursing School
15 Four-Year University or College
18 Graduate School

Age:

25 20-29 Years
13 30-39 Years
  3 Above 39 Years

Major field of study in last grade attended:

  1 Anthropology
  1 Biology
  4 Business
  1 Economics
  2 Education
  1 Health Education
  1 Human Services
  1 Industrial Design
11 Information Studies
  1 Museum Education
  4 Music
  3 Nursing
  1 Policy Administration
  1 Political Science
  2 Psychology
  1 Reading
  1 Social Science
  1 Social Work
  1 Sociology
  1 Special Education
  1 Zoology

Table 3.1 (continued)

Occupation:

1 Construction
1 Drug and Alcohol Counselor
3 Housewife
1 Industrial Designer
1 Librarian, Paraprofessional
6 Librarian, Professional
2 Museum Educator
1 Museum Volunteer
4 Musician
4 Nurse
1 Plant Security Supervisor
1 Retailing and Sales
1 School Psychologist
5 Secretary
2 Special Education and Rehabilitation
5 Student, Full-time
2 Teacher

16 (or 39%) of 41 observers reported instruction in art history. They received instruction in the following teaching environments:

8 High School
9 Four-Year University or College
1 Graduate School

Other types of art history instruction mentioned: museum course, museum docent preparation, museum visits, personal reading.

15 (or 36%) of 41 observers reported instruction in applied art. They received instruction in the following teaching environments:

3 Elementary School
3 Junior High School
7 High School
1 Junior College
2 Vocational and Technical School
5 Four-Year University or College
1 Graduate School

Other types of applied art instruction mentioned: camp, local art guild, private art instructor.

Sixteen indexers (39 percent) reported instruction in the history of art. Art history experiences beyond the high school level, reported by 10 indexers, entailed an introductory survey course and in some cases a course in a topical area. Only two reported taking more than one or two semesters of art history courses. One had taken courses in American art, ancient art, impressionism, and Egyptian art. The other had taken courses in German expressionism and Elizabethan portraiture; he was the only one to report instruction in romanesque and medieval art.

3.2.4 Indexers' Religious Background

Indexers were requested to describe any religious training or background they had that they felt helped them to describe the artworks. The denominations of the indexers were not as important as their assessments of how much their religious background contributed to the task of viewing and describing works of art. These assessments showed that 20 indexers considered that they had a weak religious background and 21 indexers considered that they had a strong religious background.

Thirteen indexers responded that they had received no religious instruction pertinent to the task. Five indexers with a Protestant background and two with a Jewish background also reported that their religious experience was not pertinent to the task. The 21 indexers who felt that they had a strong religious background described some aspects of that background that helped them perform the task of describing works of art. These indexers' statements about their strong religious background ranged from occasional Sunday school and church attendance to daily attendance at the Roman Catholic Mass and avid participation in a charismatic prayer group.

3.2.5 Identification of Primary Subject Matter

The 41 indexers followed instructions given to them and identified primary subject matter in works of art and classified their responses into objects, expressional qualities, and events.

In table 3.2 three indexers' descriptions of the primary subject matter in an artwork are consolidated into a single display; ob-

Table 3.2
Elements of Primary Subject Matter Assigned to a Work of Art by Three Indexers

Indexer	Objects	Expressional Qualities	Events
A	baby	holy	
B	man-child		reaching out
C	baby	unsure, handled with care	reaching
A	basket		
C	basket		
A	bird		
B	dove		
C	bird		
A	candle		
B	stick		
C	stick		
A	ceiling		wooden
B	woodwork		
A	cement structure	imposing	
B	stand		marble-like
C	structure		cement, coffin-like
C	eyes		
A	1 older man	happy, knowing	handing
B	man with beard	pleasant	holding
C	man	anxious, wishing	to hold, placing
A	panels		recessed
C	smile		
A	1 soldier	lurking	standing
C	man's face	mystery	looking at
A	woman	tranquil, holy	reaching out
B	woman	sacrificial	holding
C	woman	full of love	
A	2 women	nonexpressive	holding
B	woman, woman	reverential	looking, holding
C	2 women	kindness	looking on

Responses other than primary subject matter:
A "in background"   B "hidden"
A "adult-like proportions"   B "old, far beyond his size"

jects, expressional qualities, and events are enumerated in a format similar to the response form used by indexers. This display also contains responses other than primary subject matter.

3.2.6 Content Analysis of Indexers' Descriptions

For the most part, indexers identified primary subject matter in works of art. However, as table 3.2 demonstrates, they sometimes made responses that could not be considered elements of primary subject matter. The content analysis category scheme devised by Acuff and Sieber-Suppes helps in classifying and displaying these nonprimary types of responses. Content analysis categories are listed in table 3.3, followed by indexers' responses. Acuff's content analysis categories named literal object, expressive quality, hypothesis-action, hypothesis-sensation, and hypothesis-affect. These categories are not included in the table because they refer to the elements of primary subject matter. Thus examples of responses classified into Acuff's content analysis categories in table 3.3 are only nonprimary types of responses. Responses in table 3.3 serve as examples but are not comprehensive for all 100 works of art. In the process of categorizing nonprimary types of responses, we had to devise three new categories (external comparative relationship, directional, and negation) since none of Acuff's categories covered these three types of responses.

The 41 indexers formulated a total of 315 descriptions of primary subject matter. If all nonprimary responses from the 315 descriptions were categorized into Acuff's scheme, there would be approximately 375 responses. Consequently approximately one nonprimary response per description was elicited by an indexer.

Indexers who reported training in applied art or instruction in art history might be expected to refer to formal properties of art, such as materials, technique, and surface quality. So few responses were categorized into these categories, however, that no connection between indexers' art background and formal properties was attempted. Furthermore, no quantitative comparison was made because the types of art experiences reported by most individuals were not particularly extensive.

Table 3.3

Examples of Nonprimary Responses from Descriptions

I. Material attributes

    (M) Materials used in the construction of the work or that classify total work in terms of materials or medium used

gold leaf border	ornate gold leaf
canvas	frame
picture frame	plain gold frame
frame with tapestry border	massive frame

    (T) Technique, manner of application or process employed when the materials were combined

made of gold leaf	painted frame
gilt frame, medallions in bas relief	

    (SQ) Surface Quality, surface effect achieved by the combination of materials and techniques, either in terms of the textural quality of the total surface, or in terms of the textural qualities represented in special objects or areas

steely cold sword	sharp cold pointed stick
knotty cross	sharp curved sword

II. Literal Attributes

    (LC) Literal Context places subject matter with regard to time, location, events, situations

time before Christ rises from dead	after crucifixion
after having been crucified, Christ	Jesus is presented in the
has now risen	temple in Jerusalem
in the Old Testament, the scripture	Gothic arch
says this will happen after Christ	European sword
died	Middle Eastern sword

III. Sensory

    (C) Color

off-white	golden crown
black wording	chalky white faces
red tiled floor	red lips

    (L) Line, awareness of line as an identifiable element in the composition, separate from the shape which it delineates

radiating lines

(SH) Shape, statements that identify shapes or describe the dimensions or characteristic structural attributes

circular design	black blob
symmetrical cross	round object
hexagonal table	almond-shaped shell
round, dark leaf structures	T-shaped cross
pointed, diamond-shaped spear	L-shaped cross

(LT) Light, effect of light on surfaces of objects

loincloth glowing	glittering robes
shining	translucent

IV. Organizational

External comparative relationship, viewer compares specific qualities of painting with qualities not in the painting

bishop-like hat	chain-like
tree-like top on cane	demon-like child
lionish	Christ-like figure

(CR) Comparative relationship, viewer compares specific qualities or elements of painting with each other

older, more mature than other women   smaller in size than others
stand out in contrast to other buildings

(PO) Principle of Organization, awareness of the organizational principle which governs the interrelationships of one or more qualities or elements in the painting and tells how they are related

V. Expressive

(PQ) Pervasive Quality, viewer has classified the total effect of work

(US) Unique Schemata, work contains unusual or novel representations that depart from literalness and result in a total configuration that resists interpretation

appears to be floating in air   stone building out of place
strange red mountains ... very
  unreal feeling

Table 3.3 (continued)

VI. Contextual

(AF) Artform, statements that identify the type of artform at a generic level

(H/C) Historical Context, responses that indicate awareness of the temporal or cultural context in the work

(ST) Style, references to the characteristics of the work which identify a particular manner of rendering, or suggest chronological placement

stylized trees	adult-like proportions
not in perspective	old, far beyond his size

VII. Hypothesis generation

(HT) Hypothesis-Thought, hypotheses ascribing thoughts or intentions to individuals portrayed

she looks guilty or sorry	pointing as if scolding
birds sitting in basket used as sacrifice	raised as if in blessing
	two friends helping one another
man holding book as if holding an answer to secret	bald man trying to help man through crisis
woman seems to be conveying tragedy to angel	being used for learning
seems to be rising upward	looks like he planned the whole thing
looks like he got pushed down	
Mary will have a baby ...	Mary visits cousin Elizabeth and tells her she expects a baby ...
Open mouth of Gabriel says "Ave Maria, gracia plena, dominus meus"[sic]	
Lawful obedience offering the first born child and two turtle doves ...	Banner in Latin "Ave Maria"

(HNO) Hypothesis-Nature of Object, hypotheses that advance an explanation of what a person's role might be or what an object might be

tree?	scriptures?
waving sword or cloth?	Pontius Pilate?
St. Francis of Assisi?	Almighty Father?

(HC) Hypothesis-Context refers to temporal, cultural situation within which subject matter could take place

---

(HSF) Hypothesis-Subjective Feeling, hypotheses which refer to emotions elicited in the viewer by the subject matter or expressive attributes of the work.

very ominous   terrible drawing of foot
nice s-curve in banner   nice feeling of motion

(HSA) Symbolic Aspect refers to what is represented specifically functions as something else

fruit tree, tempting   thorny crown, mockery
naked--(pure)   symbolical book
woman being admired for her goodness   golden staff symbolizes
  and purity   Christ's death
skull, death, decomposing body   halos--(unity)
Father, dove, Jesus-Holy Trinity symbol   flame, symbolic of appoint-
black robe suggests death   ment by Holy Spirit
shield--(authority of king)   rocks--(hard edged reality
tenderness, promise of heaven   of this world)

(HTH) Hypothesis-Thematic identifies themes or major idea

Crucifixion   Annunciation
Birth of Christ   Transition of Christ
Sermon on the Mount   The Pierced Christ
Massacre of First-Born Babies   Creation of Eve
Visitation   Presentation

(HF) Hypothesis-Fantasy reflects the fanciful inventions of unique or novel concepts triggered by the depicted matter but only remotely related to it

Mary will be Mother of God   Mary will give birth to
                                                Jesus in Bethlehem

VIII. Contextual

   (HAR) Hypothesis-Artist, hypotheses about the intent of the artist as a personality

   (HST) Hypothesis-Style, inferences that classify the work as exemplifying a particular artist, school, or period

Table 3.3 (continued)

IX.	Affective, objective
	(AJN) Affective Judgment, Not Supported and (AJS) Affective Judgment, Supported statements judge a work in terms of the response it evokes in viewer
	none
	(OEN) Objective Evaluative, Not Supported and (OES) Objective Evaluative, Supported statements evaluate the quality of the painting as an art object
	none
X.	Negation, statements that convey that something is not depicted
	no halo no external frame
XI.	Directional statements tell where something is depicted in the work
	in the distance in background
	at left lower left
	top middle of picture bottom
	man on left left corner

Responses classified into hypothesis-thought and hypothesis-nature of object seemed similar with respect to referring to primary subject matter (for example, "tree?" or "she looks guilty or sorry") or secondary subject matter (for example, "Jesus has risen from the dead" or "Pontius Pilate?"). Concerning the former, some indexers seemed to feel a need to justify their descriptions with a story, for example, "two friends helping one another."

Indexers' responses did not fall into all of Acuff's content analysis categories. Some categories—for example, historical context, hypothesis-context, and hypothesis-style—require historical knowledge on the part of the indexer. Thus responses that would be categorized in historical context would contain some reference to the geographic area in which the artwork was produced or to the donor or commissioner of the work. Such remarks would have been out of place in this study since indexers were instructed to describe the subject matter of the works of art. Content analysis categories such as artform, principle of

organization, and pervasive quality refer to the overall characteristics of the work. Such responses would be unlikely in observers' descriptions of primary subject matter since they were
instructed to break down subject matter into three simple
elements.

The task of viewing and describing works of art entailed identifying objects, expressional qualities, and events in works of art.
There were, however, also instances of secondary subject matter
in indexers' descriptions, particularly in the descriptions of two
indexers. One of these indexers provided these secondary subject matter descriptions:

"Angel Gabriel . . . pointing upward to heaven as he announces to Mary
that she will be Mother of God."

"Dove/Holy Spirit . . . impregnating womb of Mary."

"Banner with Latin 'Ave Maria,' words of Gabriel's greeting."

"One flame dances above the head of each apostle, symbolic of appoint-
ment by the Holy Spirit."

This individual reported the following religious background:
"Twelve years of education in Catholic schools . . . fairly extensive
knowledge of New Testament." The person had also taken
courses in romanesque and medieval art.

The other indexer who described secondary subject matter
had attended a Catholic charismatic prayer group and went to
Mass daily but reported no instruction in applied art or art history. These were two of the descriptions:

"Mary visits cousin Elizabeth and tells her she expects a baby. Elizabeth
tells Mary that when she was greeting her, the child leaped into [sic] her
womb. Elizabeth will have a boy and name him John; Mary will give birth
to Jesus in Bethlehem."

"Mary will have a baby . . . open mouth of Angel Gabriel says: 'Hail Mary,
full of grace, the Lord is with you,' or 'Ave Maria, gracia plena, dominus
meus [sic].' "

Responses listed in table 3.3 for the hypothesis-thematic category describe secondary subject matter. The responses classified
in this category were culled from the descriptions of indexers

who characterized themselves as having strong and weak religious backgrounds.

We noted from indexers' descriptions that they occasionally referred to the people depicted in artworks by name, for example, "Christ" or "Elizabeth." In many instances, these identifications were correct. The naming of a person involves recognition of the person's attributes, demeanor, and physical type; consequently, such named persons were considered secondary subject matter.

A statistical test demonstrated that indexers with strong religious backgrounds were more likely to identify persons by name than were those with weak religious backgrounds (Markey, 1981). Table 3.4 lists named persons and indexers' responses expressed as primary and secondary subject matter. Notice that some persons are named incorrectly by indexers—for example, "St. Francis" instead of "God" or "Madonna" instead of "Christ." Indexers with strong or weak religious backgrounds made about the same number of errors when naming people in works of art; in this study, neither group of indexers was more prone to error.

An analysis of descriptions pointed out that indexers with strong religious backgrounds are likely to make references to secondary subject matter, but only two indexers' descriptions contained so many references to secondary subject matter as to warrant withdrawing their descriptions from the construction of the thematic catalog. These responses were set aside, and two more indexers were recruited in their place.

Indexers' descriptions of primary subject matter in medieval works of art predominantly contained references to the elements of primary subject matter (objects, expressional qualities, and events). Although there were references to formal properties of art, no connection could be made between formal properties and indexers' art background because few reported applied art training or knowledge of art history. Consequently we concluded that indexers without formal art training can be relied on to formulate descriptions to primary subject matter to medieval works of art, although the descriptions must be checked for instances of secondary subject matter. References to secondary subject matter should be replaced with their primary subject matter counterparts to ensure that descriptions of primary sub-

Table 3.4

Examples of Proper Names and Other References Used by Indexers to Name Persons Depicted in Medieval Artworks

ADAM	EVE
Adam man men-(2), included in*	Eve woman
CHRIST	GOD
angel (Christ?) body 1/2 visible Christ figure at top Jesus Jesus Christ Jesus figure lone male-(1) Madonna man (Christ) man (Jesus) man mother robe with feet transition of Christ, 1/2 robed person	Almighty Father Christ Father God God the Father God (older man) head and hands of saint man man (St. Francis of Assisi) picture of Christ St. Francis Yahweh God
CRUCIFIED THIEVES-(2)	HEROD ANTIPAS
crucified figures-(2) crucified men-(2) man on right cross, man on left cross men-(2) robbers or thieves thieves-(2)	king king (Pontius Pilate?) Pontius Pilate
	HOLY SPIRIT
	dove (dove) Holy Spirit dove symbol gull-like bird Holy Spirit in form of dove

*The phrase "included in" means that observer used a plural to describe the work, e.g., the work depicting Adam was described as "two men," so that Adam is included in the reference.

NOTE: Names in CAPITAL letters correctly identify the person(s) or figure(s) depicted. List of names following enumerates observers' attempts to name the person(s) in artworks.

Table 3.4 (continued)

INFANT CHRIST	MARY, BLESSED VIRGIN

INFANT CHRIST

    babies (Jesus?)
    baby
    baby Jesus
    cherub
    child
    child (Christ)
    child (Jesus)
    children-(2), included in
    Christ
    Christ as infant
    Christ baby
    Christ child
    child figure
    figure (angel)
    infant
    infant Christ
    Infant Jesus
    Jesus
    Jesus (baby)

JOHN THE EVANGELIST

    John
    Joseph of Arimathea
    man
    man (possibly Joseph of Arimathea)
    Mary Magdalene
    older man-(1)
    people-(4), included in
    person
    Peter
    St. John
    watchers-(2)
    woman
    women, included in
    women-(2), included in

KINGS-(3)

    kings-(3)
    men-(3)
    Wise men-(3)

MARY, BLESSED VIRGIN

    angel
    Blessed Virgin (Mary)
    central mother figure
    female saint (Virgin Mary?)
    females-(4), included to
    lady
    Madonna
    Mary
    Mary Magdalene or Virgin
    men-(13), included in
    mother
    mother figure
    Mother Mary
    persons-(2), included in
    pregnant woman
    Virgin Mary
    Virgin Mother
    watchers-(2), included in
    woman
    woman (Mary)
    women-(2), included in

MARY, BLESSED VIRGIN'S SOUL

    angel-(1), in white
    baby
    child
    infant
    Infant of Prague
    miniature person
    small figure
    small person

ST. FRANCIS OF ASSISI

    Christ (3rd)
    man on knee
    St. Thomas Aquinas

SUDARIUM

    Christ face
    face of Christ
    facial view of Christ

ject matter refer to primary subject matter and not to other aspects of the image, such as those highlighted in table 3.3.

In our experiment using medieval works of art, it was important to note indexers' background in art history, applied art, and religion. Others compiling thematic catalogs as searching aids to visual image collections such as postcard collections, newspaper photograph morgues, or public library picture collections will have to identify similar sorts of backgrounds and experiences of indexers that could affect the task. An analysis of indexers' backgrounds and responses comparable to the analysis in our experiment is suggested to ferret out indexer characteristics that are best suited to the task of formulating primary subject matter descriptions to visual images.

3.3 PREPARING COMPOSITE DESCRIPTIONS

The idea of using three indexers to describe a single work of art in this study was adopted from Firschein and Fischler (1971a, 1973) to attain completeness for the set of indexers describing the same visual image. Questions about this practice center on consistency of terminology among indexers, such as the following:

1. How often do all three indexers' terms match letter for letter?
2. How often do all three indexers' terms match, disregarding differences in terms due to synonymy or term variants?
3. Do indexers' responses agree to a greater degree when objects or expressional qualities or events are described?
4. How much of an indexer's description is unique with respect to the other two observers' descriptions?

These questions bear on the number of decisions made by the composite describer preparing composite preiconographical descriptions. For example, if indexers' responses contain fewer matches for expressional qualities than for objects, the composite describer must make more decisions to determine what terms to prefer to represent expressional qualities.

Compare the elements of primary subject matter assigned to a work of art by three indexers displayed in table 3.2. All three individuals agreed on only one term: the object "woman." In a number of instances, two of the three agreed on a term to describe primary subject matter, but on even more occasions, none of the three indexers agreed.

The degree of match between individuals' verbal descriptions of a stimulus such as a written journal article or reproduction of a work of art has been studied by various investigators for over twenty-five years in tests of interindexer consistency (Markey, 1984). We borrowed a measure from interindexer consistency tests to quantify the degree of match among the three indexers' primary subject matter descriptions of the same work of art. To determine the consistency, we had to determine what characteristics of terms constitute a match between indexers. The terms enumerated in boxes in table 3.2 can be classified into the following categories:

1. Letter-for-letter matches.
2. Single and multiple word terms.
3. Terms varying with respect to word endings.
4. Terms varying with respect to punctuation.
5. Terms varying with respect to abbreviations.
6. Spelling variants.
7. Synonyms.

Percentages of term matches were counted for terms classified into categories 1 through 7 (concept matches) and terms classified into categories 1 through 6 (terminology matches). The process of classifying terms into categories 1 through 6 can be performed automatically by computerized stemming and truncation routines. Classifying terms into category 7, synonymy, may be more difficult because the process requires computer storage and access to synonym dictionaries or look-up tables.

The number of term matches was inserted into an equation used by Slamecka and Jacoby (1965) to obtain a measure of consistency in percentage of matched terms for a group of three indexers assigning terms to sections of patents. We used their formula because it had been used in a comparable situation. Thus we could compare not only the percentage of term matches among three indexers but also their results and those of this study.

$$\text{Percentage of matching terms} = \frac{N(ABC)}{N(A) + N(B) + N(C) - N(AB) - N(AC) - N(BC) + N(ABC)}$$

where $N(A)$, $N(B)$, and $N(C)$ equal the number of terms used by each of the three indexers (indexer A, B, or C); $N(AB)$, $N(AC)$, and $N(BC)$ equal the number of terms matched between the three pairs of indexers; and $N(ABC)$ equals the number of terms matched among all three indexers.

For the artwork represented in table 3.2, we used the following numbers to derive the percentage of concept matches: $N(A) = 25$, $N(B) = 18$, $N(C) = 25$, $N(AB) = 9$, $N(AC) = 9$, $N(BC) = 9$, and $N(ABC) = 6$. Therefore:

$$\text{Percentage of concept matches} = \frac{6}{25 + 18 + 25 - 9 - 9 - 9 + 6}$$
$$= 12.8$$

For the numbers $N(A) = 25$, $N(B) = 18$, $N(C) = 25$, $N(AB) = 2$, $N(AC) = 5$, $N(BC) = 2$, and $N(ABC) = 1$,

$$\text{Percentage of terminology matches} = \frac{1}{25 + 18 + 25 - 2 - 5 - 2 + 1}$$
$$= 1.7.$$

Table 3.5 lists percentages of matching terms assigned by three indexers to 13 artworks. Each artwork was described by a different set of indexers so that the work of all 39 indexers is included in this analysis. The percentage of terminology matches is equal to or less than that of concept matches. Overall, terminology and concept matches range from 0 to 18 percent and from 6 to 21 percent, respectively. On the average, one of every eight terms elicited by all three indexers matched with respect to concept consistency; one of every fourteen terms elicited by

Table 3.5

Percentages of Matching Preiconographical Descriptors Assigned by Three Indexers*

Artwork Number	Overall	Objects	Expressional Qualities	Events
7	10 (3)	27 (8)	0	10 (0)
16	14 (4)	25 (0)	0	14 (14)
25	12 (6)	29 (9)	0	25 (14)
31	19 (18)	30 (30)	0	20 (18)
41	7 (0)	17 (0)	0	0
46	11 (7)	30 (17)	0	0
54	21 (7)	48 (14)	8 (0)	5 (4)
61	20 (14)	29 (20)	8 (8)	18 (11)
69	6 (4)	18 (13)	0	0
74	15 (11)	26 (21)	0	6 (0)
87	11 (6)	20 (13)	0	0
91	17 (7)	39 (12)	0	10 (10)
97	7 (5)	7 (6)	9 (9)	0
Range:	6-21% (0-18%)	7-48% (0-30%)	0-9% (0-9%)	0-25% (0-18%)
Average of percentages	13% (7%)	27% (13%)	2% (1%)	8% (5%)

*Numbers in parentheses refer to percentage of terminology matches between three indexers; numbers not enclosed in parentheses refer to percentage of concept matches between three indexers.

Total number of concept matches = 65
Total number of terminology matches = 41

SOURCE: Karen Markey. "Interindexer Consistency Tests: A Literature Review and report of a test of consistency in Indexing Visual Materials." Library and Information Science Research 5 (1984): 155-77.

all three indexers matched with respect to terminology consistency.

Such results should not be discouraging, however. In Slamecka and Jacoby's comparable test, where inexperienced indexers assigned terms to chemical patents without the assistance of a thesaurus, classification scheme, or controlled vocabulary, their indexers achieved consistency scores of 7.8 and 17.3 percent. A review of nearly 20 tests of interindexer consistency (Markey, 1984) demonstrated that interindexer consistency ranged from 4 to 82 percent under various conditions. Indexers in these studies had the advantage of choosing terms from the written documents themselves in contrast to observers in the present study, who had to translate visual stimuli in works of art into their corresponding verbal representations.

In view of the interindexer consistency scores among indexers in this study, the composite describer had the considerable task of analyzing three indexers' descriptions, recognizing agreement among indexers, and representing this agreement in composite descriptions. To aid the composite describer, a cross-reference and synonym dictionary was maintained. An excerpt from this dictionary is given in table 3.6. Terms used in composite descriptions are listed, accompanied by the unique number of the term used by the cluster analysis computer program and the accession number of the artwork whose composite description bears the listed term. A *see* reference indicates that the first term listed was used in an indexer's preiconographical description but the *see* reference had been preferred and employed by the composite describer when formulating the composite description of the particular work of art. As composite descriptions of new artworks were prepared, this cross-reference and synonym dictionary was continually maintained and updated by adding new terms, *see* references, and artwork accession numbers to citations, previously used terms, and *see* references.

Maintaining a cross-reference and synonym dictionary helps to control the scattering of variant terms (such as, *pierced* and *piercing*) and synonyms (for example, *pensive, anxious, thoughtful*). The problem of scatter due to interindexer consistency was especially acute in this study because many indexers were used and they worked separately, without a thesaurus.

Mischo (1979, 344) compiled a comparable cross-reference and synonym dictionary to control scatter in uncontrolled vocabulary indexes to subject-enhanced bibliographic records. He notes that "such human editing is initially time-consuming; however, the dictionary serves as a thesaurus of . . . subject terminology, and the normalization routines are less extensively employed." Thus the maintenance of a cross-reference and synonym dictionary eventually becomes less time-consuming because there are few new terms to add to the list and composite describers become familiar with preferred terms.

Table 3.6
Cross-Reference and Synonym Dictionary

Term used in composite description	(See reference to preferred term)	Cluster analysis accession no.	Artwork accession no.
overpowering	see all-knowing	2031	24
overseeing	see all-knowing	2031	23
ox	see goat	3034	54
paging		1001	1
paging		1001	30
paging		1001	47
pain, in	see suffering	2027	46
pain, in	see suffering	2027	48
pain	see suffering	2027	61
pained	see suffering	2027	13
pained	see suffering	2027	19
pale		1099	69
palm		3259	76
palms -(2)		3138	58
palms	see trees	3021	78
•			
•			
•			
pensive	see anxious	2042	21
pensive	see thoughtful	2014	25
pensive	see thoughtful	2014	34
pensive	see thoughtful	2014	57
people		3235	29
people	see men-(13)	3173	62
picking		1075	36
picture of Christ	see God	3006	1
pierced rocks	see jagged ground	3066	54
pierced with spikes	see nailed	1035	11
piercing		1094	19
piercing		1094	48
piercing		1094	80
pig		3224	40
pillar-(1)		3106	51
pillar-(1)		3106	56
pillars-(2)		3011	1
pillars-(2)		3011	69
pillars-(4)		3162	58
pillow	see cushion	3008	50
•			
•			
•			
puzzled	see bewildered	2080	75
puzzled	see questioning	2010	73

3.4 WORKING WITH CLUSTER ANALYSIS AND CLUSTERS IN CONTEXT

3.4.1 Submitting Cluster Analyses to the Computer

Overlapping cluster analysis was employed to compare the terms used in composite descriptions of primary subject matter, and the artworks to which they were assigned, to all other terms used in composite descriptions of primary subject matter and the artworks to which they were assigned. The output of the cluster analysis was a list of automatically generated groups of terms in composite descriptions. Overlapping cluster analysis allowed a term to be assigned by the cluster analysis program to more than one automatically generated group.

In the cluster analysis, 208 terms used in composite descriptions of primary subject matter, and the artworks to which they were assigned, were submitted to the computer. In practice, an individual record comprised the unique number representing the term, number of artworks whose composite descriptions contained the term, and the weights assigned to artworks.

A total of 489 unique terms were used to describe primary subject matter in the 100 works of art; however, only those terms occurring in the composite descriptions of at least three artworks were submitted to cluster analysis. Guidelines for creating clusters in context (see figure 2.8) specify that more than one term used in a similar context as another term in a composite description is needed to form a group or cluster in context. Thus a term occurring in the composite description of only one of the 100 artworks could not be used to create a cluster in context. Terms occurring in at least three artworks' composite descriptions were submitted to cluster analysis to maximize the possibility of obtaining more than one term used in a similar context as another term.

Terms used fewer than three times in composite descriptions were set aside so that the total number of terms submitted to overlapping cluster analysis was 208. A breakdown of the number of terms expressed as elements of primary subject matter showed the following:

1. Objects: Total number, 289; number used in at least three composite descriptions, 105.
2. Expressional qualities: Total number, 80; number used in at least three composite descriptions, 43.
3. Events: Total number, 120; number used in at least three composite descriptions, 60.

Because we could control certain input parameters of the clustering procedure, we made these alterations in composite descriptions during the clustering of terms:

1. MINSPLIT: The minimum number of items allowed in a vertex (or cluster) before an attempt is made to split the vertex.
2. MAXSPLIT: The maximum number of items read into the first cluster before it is allowed to split.
3. DIVIDE: The maximum number of items a vertex (or cluster) may have before it is forced to split.
4. Order of inputting incoming individual records.

Cluster analyses of terms from composite descriptions were performed 10 times. First, all 208 terms were clustered; then objects, expressional qualities, and events were clustered in the three separate analyses. Since there were so few expressional qualities (43), they were combined with 105 objects to obtain a cluster analysis of objects and expressional qualities.

These five data sets—all terms from composite descriptions, objects, expressional qualities, events, and expressional qualities and objects— were submitted to cluster analysis two times, varying with respect to input parameters. Table 3.7 lists input parameters of each cluster analysis and respective output characteristics.

Input parameters MINSPLIT and DIVIDE were initially set at 4 and 9, respectively, which allowed clusters to range from three to eight terms. These parameters were then reduced to the lowest levels—3 and 6 (or 7)— for which the cluster analysis program operated; clusters were created ranging from a minimum of two to a maximum of five (or six) terms. Only overlapping cluster analysis was used to group elements of primary subject matter so that the degree of overlap, MAXCOV, re-

Table 3.7
Cluster Analysis Input Parameters and Corresponding Characteristics of Output

INPUT

OUTPUT

No.	Random order	No. of terms	Min-split	Max-split	Divide	Max-cov	Weights	Levels of the tree	No. of vertices	No. of Overlapping items
11	All terms	208	4	12	9	1.00	none	4	63,14,3,1	145
12	Events only	60	4	12	9	1.00	none	3	18,4,1	43
13	Expressional quals.	43	4	12	9	1.00	none	3	12,4,1	18
14	Objects only	105	4	12	9	1.00	none	3	26,7,1	39
15	Objects and expressional qualities	148	4	12	9	1.00	none	4	46,11,3,1	111
16	Objects only	105	3	6	6	1.00	none	4	31,9,3,1	21
17	Expressional quals.	43	3	7	7	1.00	none	3	15,6,1	24
18	All Terms	208	3	6	6	1.00	none	5	73,22,8,4,1	77
19	Objects and expressional qualities	148	3	7	7	1.00	none	4	48,14,5,1	72
20	Events only	60	3	7	7	1.00	none	3	20,6,1	19

mained at its highest level (100 percent overlap) throughout the 10 cluster analyses of terms from composite descriptions.

Clustering terms from composite descriptions provides raw output of groups of terms, which must be examined and organized into clusters in context. In clusters in context, grouped terms are reinstated into the English-language phrases and sentences in the preiconographical descriptions from which they were extracted. This procedure is necessary to provide readers of grouped terms with the context of terms in relation to other terms.

3.4.2 Creating Clusters in Context

Clustering terms from composite descriptions resulted in tree structures ranging from three to five levels. Clusters in context were created from the lowest and second-lowest levels of the tree structure. The number of lowest-level vertices was 352; the number of second-lowest level vertices was 97. If every automatically generated group of terms on the lowest level of the tree comprised a cluster in context, 352 clusters in context would have been created. If every automatically generated group of terms on the second-lowest level of the tree structure comprised a cluster in context, 97 clusters in context would have been created. Some automatically generated groups of terms, however, failed to comprise clusters in context, for the following reasons:

1. Composite descriptions of artworks contained half or less than half of the clustered terms.
2. When artworks whose composite descriptions contained at least more than half of the clustered terms were singled out, the use of these terms in the context of the composite description was not deemed similar.
3. At least three-quarters of the descriptive phrases of one cluster in context duplicated descriptive phrases in another cluster in context.

3.4.3 Secondary Meaning of Clusters in Context

Three iconographers, recruited at Cornell University's Department of the History of Art, read 65 clusters in context and were instructed to identify the secondary subject matter delineated by the cluster in context. Each iconographer received a packet containing instructions and 65 clusters in context. When compiling clusters in context, we noticed that certain clusters in context almost duplicated one another or that certain descriptive phrases occurred repeatedly from one cluster in context to another. Feeling that iconographers might carry over what they learned from examining one cluster in context to subsequent ones, we instructed iconographers to read each cluster in context as it appeared in a page-by-page arrangement and respond without referring to clusters in context preceding or following.

The iconographers examined the clusters in context one at a time, named the theme that the cluster in context expressed, and, if they encountered difficulties, reported the nature of the difficulties. The iconographers did not have recourse to any visual representations of the clusters in context. In 33 of 65 instances of naming clusters in context, all three iconographers agreed about the specific theme cited by descriptive phrases of the clusters in context. Two of the three agreed about the theme in the case of 13 other clusters in context. In three clusters in context, the iconographers agreed that although one theme predominated, elements of another identifiable theme were present. Agreement among iconographers concerning whether clusters in context did or did not refer to a theme was usually evident. Examining iconographers' responses to naming the theme cited by clusters in context revealed five categories of 65 clusters in context:

A. One theme is described by the descriptive phrases of the cluster in context.

B. One identifiable theme predominates in the cluster in context, but descriptive phrases referring to other themes can be singled out.

C. No one theme predominates; descriptive phrases refer to two or more themes.

D. The cluster in context does not convey enough information to describe any theme.

E. The cluster in context does not describe a theme.

One example of a cluster in context from each of these categories is presented in appendix B.

A thematic catalog of primary and secondary subject matter can be compiled from clusters in context exhibiting characteristics A or B. In these two cases, the descriptive phrases identify elements of preiconographical description, or primary subject matter, and the theme designates secondary subject matter.

The number of clusters exhibiting characteristics A or B is presented in table 3.8, along with clusters in context presented to iconographers from all 10 cluster analyses and the number of clusters in context exhibiting characteristics A or B from all 10 cluster analyses. Clusters in context suitable for the thematic catalog resulted from all 10 cluster analyses.

It is doubtful that the 10 cluster analyses of preiconographical descriptors performed in this study exhausted all possible groupings of terms. Additional cluster analyses of objects, events, and expressional qualities, and combinations of these, particularly with input parameters different from those used in this study, may yield more clusters in context for the thematic catalog.

These cluster analysis results are unique to the set of artworks used in this experiment. Other researchers and practitioners using cluster analysis programs to compile thematic catalogs of primary and secondary subject matter will have to adjust to the idiosyncrasies of the cluster analysis program selected by adjusting their input parameters and submitting a number of cluster analyses to the computer. Our experiment was exploratory in that it tested the process of compiling a thematic catalog and led to recommendations for refining that process.

Table 3.8
Clusters in Context from 10 Cluster Analyses of Terms That Contributed to the Thematic Catalog

Cluster analysis no. (corresponding to Table 3.7)	Total no. of clusters in context	No. of clusters in context from lowest-level vertices exhibiting characteristic A or B	Total no. of clusters in context from lowest-level vertices	No. of clusters in context from second level vertices exhibiting characteristic A or B	Total no. of clusters in context from second lowest level vertices	Total no. of clusters in context contributing to Thematic Catalog (exhibiting characteristic A or B)	Input Parameters
11. All 208 terms	8	3	4	2	4	5	Minsplit=4
12. 60 Events only	4	0	1	2	3	2	Divide=9 Maxsplit=12
13. 43 Expressional qualities	2	2	2	0	0	2	
14. 105 Objects only	7	4	4	2	3	6	71% of clusters in context contributing to Thematic Catalog (analyses 11–15)
15. 43 Expressional qualities and 105 objects	13	8	12	1	1	9	
16. 105 Objects only	8	4	5	3	3	7	Minsplit=3 Divide=6 or 7 Maxsplit=6 or 7
17. 43 Expressional qualities	2	1	1	0	1	1	
18. All 208 terms	7	5	6	1	1	6	81% of clusters in context contributing to Thematic Catalog (analyses 16–20)
19. 43 Expressional qualities and 105 objects	8	3	3	3	5	6	
20. 60 Events only	6	3	4	2	2	5	
Total	65	33	42	16	23	49	or 75% of clusters in context contributing to the Thematic Catalog

4 A Thematic Catalog of Primary and Secondary Subject Matter

4.1 REVIEW OF COMPILING A THEMATIC CATALOG

The process of compiling a thematic catalog of primary and secondary subject matter entails eight steps, depicted in flowchart format in figure 3.1. The first step entails the selection of artworks and observers. In our study, 100 works of art executed in Northern Europe between 1250 and 1425 were selected. Thus the thematic catalog compiled in this study is specific to the geographical area and chronological time period represented by the works of art. Observers who had a minimum of training in applied art, religious history, and art history were chosen. The observers described primary subject matter (objects, expressional qualities, and events) in the 100 works of art. To ensure completeness, we obtained descriptions of the primary subject matter in a single work of art from three observers. In the third step of the process, these three descriptions per work of art were consolidated into a single composite description by a composite describer.

In the fourth step, overlapping cluster analysis was used to automatically generate groups of terms used to represent primary subject matter in preiconographical descriptions. In step 5, grouped terms were reinstated into the context of the composite description in which they occurred. The result of step 5 was the creation of clusters in context which, in steps 6 and 7 were given to iconographers who reviewed the clusters in context to identify their secondary meaning. Whenever iconographers linked clusters in context to their secondary meaning, the clusters and their respective secondary meaning were used to compile a thematic catalog of primary and secondary subject matter. Compiling the thematic catalog is the eighth and culminating step in the process.

This chapter highlights the thematic catalog of primary and secondary subject matter that was compiled from observers' descriptions of 100 late medieval artworks and iconographers' descriptions of the works' secondary meaning. Preceding the catalog is an introduction that explains the catalog's layout and identifies potential users and uses of the catalog.

4.2 INTRODUCTION TO THE THEMATIC CATALOG OF PRIMARY AND SECONDARY SUBJECT MATTER IN LATE MEDIEVAL ART

The history of art is marked by few occasions when the representational elements and the theme of a work of art coincide. For example, the artists' depictions of subject matter—a pot of sunflowers, a landscape, or a crowded theater—mean just a pot of sunflowers, a landscape, or a crowded theater during brief periods in the history of Western Art. But this is the exception rather than the rule, and at no other time is the rule better exemplified than during the late medieval era. Describing a medieval work of art on the representational level, we identify a "male figure holding fruit" as one of many representational elements. But "male holding fruit" is a relatively general description. Does it symbolize St. Sabas, who is regularly depicted holding an apple, or the Fall of Man, in which Adam is likely to be holding the infamous apple presented to him by Eve? To link these representational elements with their symbolic implication, we must have acquired knowledge of biblical events and the history of the Christian church. Such knowledge is the province of those who have been trained in iconography, the study of subject matter or meaning in art.

Aiding scholars to pursue iconographical studies, centers of

documentation have developed research collections of reproductions of works of art; examples are the Index of Christian
Art at Princeton University and the Decimal Index to Art in the
Low Countries at the Netherlands Institute for Art History. The
subject matter of works of art contained in these collections has
been described along the lines of symbolic implications, so successful access to these collections is limited to those trained in
the study of iconography.

The thematic catalog is an example of a searching aid to iconographical research collections covering late medieval Northern
European art. Its purpose is to help users of these iconographical
research collections who do not know the symbolic implications
of artworks' representational elements. This aid seeks to bring
together a listing of symbolic themes and concepts. Consulting
the searching aid, users can translate representational elements
into the appropriate symbolic theme or concept and then search
the iconographical collection at hand. Searchers of iconographical research collections who are potential users of the thematic
catalog may be involved in disciplines closely related to medieval
art history, such as the history of science, musical iconography,
and medieval studies. Students of art history may find the catalog
useful when identifying a particularly elusive theme. Art histo-
rians are encouraged to consult the catalog when researching
unfamiliar subjects.

4.3 HOW TO USE THE THEMATIC CATALOG

The catalog comprises two sections: (1) an alphabetical enumeration of primary subject matter in a keyword-in-context format and the corresponding secondary meaning and (2) an
alphabetical directory of secondary subject matter and the elements of primary subject matter of which it is constituted. Consulting the first portion of the thematic catalog, searchers can
identify the secondary meaning of the representational elements
they have in mind and then search the iconographical research
collection at hand.

As an example, consider a search for "Musical Instruments."
The researcher looks for "Musical Instruments" in the first sec-

tion of the thematic catalog, which enumerates primary subject matter in an alphabetically arranged keyword-in-context display. The "M" section of the thematic catalog shows these listings:

> one of *men-(12)* sitting with book
> DEATH OF VIRGIN
> three of *men-(12)* crouching, reading book
> DEATH OF VIRGIN
> angels-(2) playing *musical instrument*
> NATIVITY
> joyous angels-(3) playing *musical instrument*
> NATIVITY
> Christ *nailed* to cross-(1)
> CRUCIFIXION

In this example, the italicized words are elements of primary subject matter. The researcher will see that "Musical Instrument" is depicted in images of the Nativity. Turning to "Nativity" in the second subject matter section of the catalog, the researcher now can find other elements of primary subject matter depicted in scenes of the Nativity. Before searching the iconographical research collection for visual images of musical instruments, the user might want to check under specific names of musical instruments (such as *lute, recorder*, or *zither*) in the catalog to collect other themes in which musical instruments are depicted.

The usefulness of the directory to secondary meaning is best exemplified for those who are unfamiliar with the identity of a particular theme and can compare the illustration with the descriptive phrases of a secondary theme. For example, a user might be unfamiliar with a scene in which one man is praying and three others are sleeping in a rocky landscape. Consulting the primary subject matter compilation of the catalog, he or she finds the phrase "men-(3) sleeping..." and is directed to the theme "Agony in the Garden." Under "Agony in the Garden" in the secondary subject matter compilation are listed elements that coincide with others of interest in this search. For example, the "man praying" may be "Christ kneeling and praying on hill," and the "rocky landscape" matches with references to "cliff and trees," "hill and trees," and "trees, jagged ground and hill."

4.4 PRIMARY SUBJECT MATTER

The primary subject matter portion of the thematic catalog lists preiconographical descriptors in an alphabetical, keyword-in-context format. Only a portion of the alphabet is given here. Preiconographical descriptors from "Infant Christ" to "Standing" comprise the primary subject matter portion of the thematic catalog. This portion serves as an example of primary subject matter in the thematic catalog to provide an idea of its content and format and relationship to the secondary subject matter portion.

Sample Thematic Catalog

PRIMARY SUBJECT MATTER	SECONDARY SUBJECT MATTER
•	•
•	•
•	•
Infant Christ and dove-(1) flying	ANNUNCIATION
Infant Christ clutching bird-(1) in hand-(1)	MADONNA AND CHILD
Infant Christ holding bird-(1) in hand-(1)	MADONNA AND CHILD
Mary holding *Infant Christ*	ADORATION OF THE MAGI
angel-(1) with wings-(2) *instructing* Mary	ANNUNCIATION
angel-(1) with wings-(2) *instructing* Mary, pointing finger-(1)	ANNUNCIATION
forceful angel-(1) *instructing* with arm-(1) outstretched	ANNUNCIATION
forceful angel-(1) *instructing* with finger-(1) pointing	ANNUNCIATION
angels-(3) playing musical *instrument*	NATIVITY
joyous angels-(2) playing musical *instrument*	NATIVITY
men-(3) sleeping and sitting on *jagged ground*	AGONY IN THE GARDEN

PRIMARY SUBJECT MATTER	SECONDARY SUBJECT MATTER
trees, *jagged ground* and hill	AGONY IN THE GARDEN
Mary wearing *jeweled* crown	MADONNA AND CHILD
Joseph, thoughtful, leaning on cane	NATIVITY
Joseph with canteen hanging from belt	NATIVITY
Joseph with pouch hanging from belt	NATIVITY
joyous angels-(2) playing musical instrument	NATIVITY
elderly man with pouch and *key* hanging from belt	NATIVITY
kings-(3) with crown offering gifts	ADORATION OF THE MAGI
angel-(1) *kneeling* before Mary	ANNUNCIATION
Christ *kneeling* and praying on hill	AGONY IN THE GARDEN
haloed angel-(1), gentle, *kneeling* before Mary	ANNUNCIATION
haloed Mary surprised *kneeling* at lectern	ANNUNCIATION
Mary *kneeling* at lectern	ANNUNCIATION
Mary *kneeling* at lectern before open books-(2)	ANNUNCIATION
Mary *kneeling* at lectern, paging through open books-(2)	ANNUNCIATION

Sample Thematic Catalog (continued)

PRIMARY SUBJECT MATTER	SECONDARY SUBJECT MATTER
undersized man-(1) and woman-(1) *kneeling* and praying	CRUCIFIXION
...	CRUCIFIXION WITH DONOR PORTRAITS
	AGONY IN THE GARDEN
men-(3) with arms-(2) folded on *knees*	CRUCIFIXION
man-(1) sitting with book-(1) on *lap*	ADORATION OF THE MAGI
Mary holding Infant Christ on *lap*	NATIVITY
Joseph, thoughtful, *leaning* on cane	ANNUNCIATION
haloed Mary surprised kneeling at *lectern*	ANNUNCIATION
haloed Mary surprised standing at *lectern*	ANNUNCIATION
Mary kneeling at *lectern*	ANNUNCIATION
Mary kneeling at *lectern* before open books-(2)	ANNUNCIATION
Mary kneeling at *lectern* paging through open books-(2)	ANNUNCIATION
Mary standing at *lectern*	ANNUNCIATION
Mary *listening* and standing	

PRIMARY SUBJECT MATTER	SECONDARY SUBJECT MATTER
Christ dressed in *loincloth*	CRUCIFIXION
...	CRUCIFIXION WITH MARY AND ST. JOHN MAN OF SORROWS
...	ENTOMBMENT
men-(2), *loving*, placing Christ in casket	ENTOMBMENT
Christ *lying* on open casket	DEATH OF THE VIRGIN
haloed woman-(1) *lying* in bed, calm	DEATH OF THE VIRGIN
haloed woman-(1) *lying* in bed, sorrowful	NATIVITY
Mary *lying* in bed	CRUCIFIXION
man-(1) dressed in red gown	CRUCIFIXION
man-(1) dressed in red gown, standing	CRUCIFIXION
man-(1) grieving, arms-(2) upraised	CRUCIFIXION WITH LONGINUS
...	

Sample Thematic Catalog (continued)

PRIMARY SUBJECT MATTER	SECONDARY SUBJECT MATTER
man-*(1)* holding book-(1) gazing at Christ	CRUCIFIXION
...	CRUCIFIXION WITH MARY AND ST. JOHN
man-*(1)* observant with outstretched arm-(1)	ANNUNCIATION
man-*(1)* piercing chest of Christ with spear-(1)	CRUCIFIXION
...	CRUCIFIXION WITH LONGINUS AND STEPHATON
man-*(1)* pointing finger-(1) at Christ	CRUCIFIXION
man-*(1)* sitting with book-(1) in lap	CRUCIFIXION
man-*(1)* standing dressed in red gown	CRUCIFIXION
man-*(1)* standing holding book-(1)	CRUCIFIXION
man-*(1)* standing with arm-(1) upraised	CRUCIFIXION
...	CRUCIFIXION WITH DONOR PORTRAITS
...	CRUCIFIXION WITH MARY AND ST. JOHN
man-*(1)* standing with hand-(1) upraised	CRUCIFIXION
...	CRUCIFIXION WITH MARY AND ST. JOHN

PRIMARY SUBJECT MATTER	SECONDARY SUBJECT MATTER
man-(1) standing with hands-(2) upraised	CRUCIFIXION
...	CRUCIFIXION WITH DONOR PORTRAITS
...	CRUCIFIXION WITH MARY AND ST. JOHN
man-(1) supporting Mary	CRUCIFIXION
...	CRUCIFIXION WITH MARY AND ST. JOHN
	NATIVITY
elderly man- with pouch and key hanging from belt	CRUCIFIXION
undersized man-(1) and woman-(1) kneeling and praying	CRUCIFIXION WITH DONOR PORTRAITS
...	ENTOMBMENT
women-(2), man-(1) and Mary standing	CRUCIFIXION
Mary dressed in black gown	CRUCIFIXION WITH LONGINUS AND STEPHATON
...	CRUCIFIXION WITH MARY AND ST. JOHN
...	

Sample Thematic Catalog (continued)

PRIMARY SUBJECT MATTER	SECONDARY SUBJECT MATTER
Mary dressed in blue gown, thoughtful	CRUCIFIXION
Mary dressed in blue gown, weeping	CRUCIFIXION
Mary dressed in ornate gown	ADORATION OF THE MAGI
Mary grieving, touching Christ's hand-(1)	ENTOMBMENT
Mary holding book-(1)	ANNUNCIATION
Mary holding Infant Christ in her arm-(1)	MADONNA AND CHILD
Mary holding Infant Christ in her lap	MADONNA AND CHILD
Mary kneeling at lectern	ANNUNCIATION
Mary kneeling at lectern before open books-(2)	ANNUNCIATION
Mary kneeling at lectern paging through open books-(2)	ANNUNCIATION
Mary listening and standing	ANNUNCIATION
Mary lying in bed	NATIVITY
Mary lying in straw bed	NATIVITY

PRIMARY SUBJECT MATTER	SECONDARY SUBJECT MATTER
Mary paging through open books-(2)	ANNUNCIATION
Mary sitting on ornate throne	ADORATION OF THE MAGI
...	ANNUNCIATION
...	MADONNA AND CHILD
Mary sitting on throne	ADORATION OF THE MAGI
...	ANNUNCIATION
...	MADONNA AND CHILD
Mary, sorrowful, dressed in black gown	CRUCIFIXION
Mary, sorrowful, standing	CRUCIFIXION
Mary, sorrowful, supported by women-(1)	CRUCIFIXION
...	CRUCIFIXION WITH DONOR PORTRAITS
Mary, sorrowful, supported by women-(3)	CRUCIFIXION

Sample Thematic Catalog (continued)

PRIMARY SUBJECT MATTER	SECONDARY SUBJECT MATTER
Mary, sorrowful, weeping	CRUCIFIXION
Mary standing at lectern	ANNUNCIATION
Mary standing silent and grieving	ENTOMBMENT
Mary touching her chest with hand-(1)	ANNUNCIATION
Mary with bloodstains on veil	CRUCIFIXION
...	CRUCIFIXION WITH LONGINUS AND STEPHATON
...	CRUCIFIXION WITH MARY AND ST. JOHN
Mary with hands-(2) crossed	CRUCIFIXION
Mary with head inclined	CRUCIFIXION
angel-(1) kneeling before Mary	ANNUNCIATION
angel-(1) stepping towards Mary	ANNUNCIATION
angel-(1) with wings-(2) instructing Mary, pointing finger-(1)	ANNUNCIATION
haloed angel-(1), gentle, kneeling before Mary	ANNUNCIATION

PRIMARY SUBJECT MATTER	SECONDARY SUBJECT MATTER
haloed angel-(1), gentle, stepping towards *Mary*	ANNUNCIATION
haloed *Mary* surprised kneeling at lectern	ANNUNCIATION
haloed *Mary* surprised standing at lectern	ANNUNCIATION
man-(1) supporting *Mary*	CRUCIFIXION
...	CRUCIFIXION WITH MARY AND ST. JOHN
women-(2) and *Mary* standing	ENTOMBMENT
women-(2), man-(1) and *"Mary"* standing	ENTOMBMENT
men-(2), loving, placing Christ in casket	ENTOMBMENT
one of men-(2) offering stick with sponge to Christ	CRUCIFIXION
...	CRUCIFIXION WITH LONGINUS AND STEPHATON
...	CRUCIFIXION WITH STEPHATON

89

Sample Thematic Catalog (continued)

PRIMARY SUBJECT MATTER	SECONDARY SUBJECT MATTER
one of *men–(2)* piercing chest of Christ with spear–(1)	CRUCIFIXION
...	CRUCIFIXION WITH LONGINUS
...	CRUCIFIXION WITH LONGINUS AND STEPHATON
men–(2) tied to crosses–(2)	CRUCIFIXION
men–(3) sleeping and sitting on jagged ground	AGONY IN THE GARDEN
men–(3) sleeping, crouching in grass	AGONY IN THE GARDEN
men–(3) sleeping with arms–(2) folded on knees	AGONY IN THE GARDEN
men–(3) with arms–(2) folded on knees	AGONY IN THE GARDEN
one of *men–(12)* holding book–(1)	DEATH OF THE VIRGIN
one of *men–(12)* sitting with book–(1)	DEATH OF THE VIRGIN
three of *men–(12)* crouching and reading book–(1)	DEATH OF THE VIRGIN

PRIMARY SUBJECT MATTER	SECONDARY SUBJECT MATTER
cross-(1) standing upright on *mound*	CRUCIFIXION
...	CRUCIFIXION WITH DONOR PORTRAITS
...	CRUCIFIXION WITH LONGINUS
...	CRUCIFIXION WITH MARY AND ST. JOHN
angels-(3) playing *musical instrument*	NATIVITY
joyous angels-(2) playing *musical instrument*	NATIVITY
Christ, dead, *nailed*	CRUCIFIXION
Christ *nailed* on cross-(1)	CRUCIFIXION
...	CRUCIFIXION WITH DCNOR PORTRAITS
...	CRUCIFIXION WITH LONGINUS
...	CRUCIFIXION WITH LONGINUS AND STEPHATON
...	CRUCIFIXION WITH MARY AND ST. JOHN
...	CRUCIFIXION WITH STEPHATON
Christ, sad, *nailed* on cross-(1)	CRUCIFIXION

Sample Thematic Catalog (continued)

PRIMARY SUBJECT MATTER	SECONDARY SUBJECT MATTER
Christ, suffering, *nailed* on cross-(1)	CRUCIFIXION
...	CRUCIFIXION WITH ESTAB-LISHMENT OF THE CHURCH CRUCIFIXION WITH LONGINUS
...	CRUCIFIXION
plaque *nailed* on cross-(1)	CRUCIFIXION WITH MARY AND ST. JOHN
God *observant* beckoning with outstretched hand-(1)	ANNUNCIATION
God *observant* sending in outstretched hands-(2)	ANNUNCIATION
man-(1) *observant* with outstretched arm-(1)	ANNUNCIATION
kings-(3) with crown *offering* gifts	ADORATION OF THE MAGI
one of men-(2) *offering* stick with sponge to Christ	CRUCIFIXION
...	CRUCIFIXION WITH LONGINUS AND STEPHATON
...	CRUCIFIXION WITH STEPHATON

PRIMARY SUBJECT MATTER | SECONDARY SUBJECT MATTER

PRIMARY SUBJECT MATTER	SECONDARY SUBJECT MATTER
one of soldiers *offering* stick with sponge to Christ	CRUCIFIXION
onlookers	CRUCIFIXION
...	CRUCIFIXION WITH LONGINUS
onlookers disinterested	CRUCIFIXION
...	CRUCIFIXION WITH LONGINUS
onlookers standing	CRUCIFIXION
sad *onlookers*	CRUCIFIXION
Mary kneeling at lectern before *open books-(2)*	ANNUNCIATION
Mary kneeling at lectern paging through *open books-(2)*	ANNUNCIATION
Mary paging through *open books-(2)*	ANNUNCIATION
Christ lying on *open casket*	ENTOMBMENT
Christ sitting on *open casket*	RESURRECTION
men-(2) placing Christ in *open casket*	ENTOMBMENT
Christ standing in front of *open casket*	RESURRECTION

93

Sample Thematic Catalog (continued)

PRIMARY SUBJECT MATTER	SECONDARY SUBJECT MATTER
Mary dressed in *ornate gown*	MADONNA AND CHILD
Mary sitting on *ornate throne*	ANNUNCIATION
Mary, unsure, sitting on *ornate throne*	ANNUNCIATION
woman—(1) sitting on *ornate throne*	ANNUNCIATION
woman—(1), unsure, sitting on *ornate throne*	ANNUNCIATION
Christ hanging on cross—(1) with arms—(2) *outstretched*	CRUCIFIXION
Christ with arms—(2) *outstretched* and bleeding	CRUCIFIXION WITH ESTAB-LISHMENT OF THE CHURCH
forceful angel—(1) instructing with arm—(1) *outstretched*	ANNUNCIATION
God observant beckoning with *outstretched* hand—(1)	ANNUNCIATION
God observant sending in *outstretched* hands—(2)	ANNUNCIATION
man—(1) observant with *outstretched* arm—(1)	ANNUNCIATION
Mary *paging* through open books—(2)	ANNUNCIATION
Mary kneeling at lectern *paging* through open books—(2)	ANNUNCIATION

PRIMARY SUBJECT MATTER	SECONDARY SUBJECT MATTER
man-(1) *piercing* chest of Christ with spear-(1)	CRUCIFIXION
...	CRUCIFIXION WITH LONGINUS AND STEPHATON
one of men-(2) *piercing* chest of Christ with spear-(1)	CRUCIFIXION
...	CRUCIFIXION WITH LONGINUS
...	CRUCIFIXION WITH LONGINUS AND STEPHATON
one of soldiers *piercing* chest of Christ with spear-(1)	CRUCIFIXION
...	CRUCIFIXION WITH LONGINUS
...	CRUCIFIXION WITH LONGINUS AND STEPHATON
men-(2) *placing* Christ in open casket	ENTOMBMENT
plaque nailed to cross-(1)	CRUCIFIXION
...	CRUCIFIXION WITH DONOR PORTRAITS
...	CRUCIFIXION WITH MARY AND ST. JOHN

Sample Thematic Catalog (continued)

PRIMARY SUBJECT MATTER	SECONDARY SUBJECT MATTER
angels-(3) *playing* musical instrument	NATIVITY
joyous angels-(2) *playing* musical instrument	NATIVITY
angel-(1) with wings-(2) instructing Mary, *pointing* finger-(1)	ANNUNCIATION
angel-(1) with wings-(2) *pointing* finger-(1) at Christ	CRUCIFIXION
forceful angel-(1) instructing with finger-(1) *pointing*	ANNUNCIATION
man-(1) *pointing* finger-(1) at Christ	CRUCIFIXION
one of soldiers *pointing* finger-(1) at Christ	CRUCIFIXION
elderly man with *pouch* and key hanging from belt	NATIVITY
Joseph with *pouch* hanging from belt	NATIVITY
Christ kneeling and *praying* on hill	AGONY IN THE GARDEN
undersized man-(1) and woman-(1) kneeling and *praying*	CRUCIFIXION
...	CRUCIFIXION WITH DONOR PORTRAITS

96

PRIMARY SUBJECT MATTER	SECONDARY SUBJECT MATTER
three of men-(12) crouching and *reading* book-(1)	DEATH OF THE VIRGIN
man-(1) dressed in *red gown*	CRUCIFIXION
...	CRUCIFIXION WITH LCNGINUS
...	CRUCIFIXION WITH MARY AND ST. JOHN
sad onlookers	CRUCIFIXION
Christ, *sad*, hanging on cross-(1)	CRUCIFIXION
...	CRUCIFIXION WITH LONGINUS
Christ, *sad*, nailed on cross-(1)	CRUCIFIXION
...	CRUCIFIXION WITH DONOR PORTRAITS
God observant *sending* in outstretched hands-(2)	ANNUNCIATION
Christ wrapped in *sheer* cloth	ENTOMBMENT
Mary standing *silent* and grieving	ENTOMBMENT
Christ *sitting* on open casket	RESURRECTION

Sample Thematic Catalog (continued)

PRIMARY SUBJECT MATTER	SECONDARY SUBJECT MATTER
man-(1) *sitting* with book-(1) in lap	CRUCIFIXION
Mary *sitting* on ornate throne	ANNUNCIATION
...	MADONNA AND CHILD
Mary, unsure, *sitting* on ornate throne	ANNUNCIATION
men-(3) sleeping and *sitting* on jagged ground	AGONY IN THE GARDEN
one of men-(12) *sitting* with book-(1)	DEATH OF THE VIRGIN
woman-(1) *sitting* on ornate throne	ANNUNCIATION
woman-(1), unsure, *sitting* on ornate throne	ANNUNCIATION
men-(3) *sleeping* and sitting on jagged ground	AGONY IN THE GARDEN
men-(3) *sleeping*, crouching in grass	AGONY IN THE GARDEN
men-(3) *sleeping* with arms-(2) folded on knees	AGONY IN THE GARDEN

PRIMARY SUBJECT MATTER	SECONDARY SUBJECT MATTER
soldiers holding weapon	CRUCIFIXION
one of *soldiers* offering stick with sponge to Christ	CRUCIFIXION
...	CRUCIFIXION WITH LONGINUS AND STEPHATON
...	CRUCIFIXION WITH STEPHATON
one of *soldiers* piercing chest of Christ with spear-(1)	CRUCIFIXION
...	CRUCIFIXION WITH LONGINUS
...	CRUCIFIXION WITH LONGINUS AND STEPHATON
one of *soldiers* pointing finger-(1) at Christ	CRUCIFIXION
soldiers surprised and afraid, crouching on ground	RESURRECTION
soldiers surprised sitting on ground	RESURRECTION
haloed woman-(1) lying on bed, *sorrowful*	DEATH OF THE VIRGIN
Mary, *sorrowful*, dressed in black gown	CRUCIFIXION
Mary, *sorrowful*, standing	CRUCIFIXION

Sample Thematic Catalog (continued)

PRIMARY SUBJECT MATTER	SECONDARY SUBJECT MATTER
Mary, *sorrowful*, supported by woman–(1)	CRUCIFIXION
...	CRUCIFIXION WITH DONOR PORTRAITS
Mary, *sorrowful*, supported by women–(3)	CRUCIFIXION
woman–(1), *sorrowful*, dressed in black gown	CRUCIFIXION
woman–(1), *sorrowful*, standing	CRUCIFIXION
Mary, *sorrowful*, weeping	CRUCIFIXION
man–(1) piercing chest of Christ with *spear–(1)*	CRUCIFIXION WITH LONGINUS AND STEPHATON
...	CRUCIFIXION
one of men–(2) piercing chest of Christ with *spear–(1)*	CRUCIFIXION WITH LONGINUS
...	CRUCIFIXION WITH LONGINUS AND STEPHATON
one of soldiers piercing chest of Christ with *spear–(1)*	CRUCIFIXION
...	CRUCIFIXION WITH LONGINUS
...	CRUCIFIXION WITH LONGINUS AND STEPHATON

PRIMARY SUBJECT MATTER

one of men-(2) offering stick with *sponge* to Christ

. . .

. . .

one of soldiers offering stick with *sponge* to Christ

. . .

. . .

wooden *stable*

Christ *standing* in front of open casket

man-(1) *standing* dressed in red gown

• • •

SECONDARY SUBJECT MATTER

CRUCIFIXION

CRUCIFIXION WITH LONGINUS
AND STEPHATON
CRUCIFIXION WITH STEPHATON

CRUCIFIXION

CRUCIFIXION WITH LONGINUS
AND STEPHATON
CRUCIFIXION WITH STEPHATON

NATIVITY

RESURRECTION

CRUCIFIXION

• • •

4.5 SECONDARY SUBJECT MATTER

Here we provide as an example six of the 10 secondary themes. Each secondary theme is named and accompanied by descriptive phrases and preiconographical descriptors in an alphabetical, keyword-in-context format. These six themes serve as an example of secondary subject matter in the thematic catalog to show its content and format and relationship to the primary subject matter portion. The entire Thematic Catalog of Primary and Secondary Subject Matter in Medieval Art is four times the length of the two thematic catalog portions in this chapter (Markey, 1981).

Mary holding Infant Christ in her *arm-(1)* and lap

Mary holding Infant *Christ*

kings-(3) wearing *crown*

Mary wearing *crown*

kings-(3) with crown offering *gifts*

kings-(3) offering gifts in *hand-(1)*

Mary touching Christ's *hand-(1)* with hers

Mary holding *Infant Christ*

kings-(3) with crown offering gifts

Mary holding Infant Christ on *lap*

Mary sitting on ornate throne

Mary sitting on throne

kings-(3) with crown *offering gifts*

Mary dressed in *ornate gown*

Mary sitting on *throne*

AGONY IN THE GARDEN

men-(3) with *arms*-(2) folded on knees

    Christ kneeling and praying on hill

    cliff and trees

men-(3) sleeping, *crouching* in grass

men-(3) with arms-(2) *folded* on knees

men-(3) sleeping, crouching in *grass*

men-(3) sleeping and sitting on jagged *ground*

    trees, jagged *ground* and hill

Christ kneeling and praying on *hill*

    trees and *hill*

men-(3) sleeping and sitting on *jagged ground*

    trees, *jagged ground* and hill

    Christ *kneeling* and praying on hill

men-(3) with arms-(2) folded on *knees*

men-(3)   sleeping and sitting on jagged ground

men-(3)   sleeping, crouching in grass

men-(3)   sleeping with arms-(2) folded on knees

men-(3)   with arms-(2) folded on knees

Christ kneeling and *praying*   on hill

men-(3) sleeping and *sitting*   on jagged ground

men-(3)   *sleeping* and sitting on jagged ground

men-(3)   *sleeping*, crouching in grass

men-(3)   *sleeping* with arms-(2) folded on knees

cliff and *trees*

hill and *trees*

trees, jagged ground and hill

Christ with	*angels-(4)* flying, one holding chalice up to Christ
woman-(1) dressed in	*arms-(2)* outstretched and bleeding
Christ	*black gown*
	bleeding from hands-(2), feet and gash in chest
Christ with arms-(2) outstretched and	*bleeding*
angels-(4) flying, one holding	*chalice* up to Christ
Christ bleeding from hands-(2), feet and gash in	*chest*
	Christ bleeding from hands-(2), feet and gash in chest
	Christ, suffering, nailed on cross-(1)
	Christ with arms-(2) outstretched and bleeding
angels-(4) flying, one holding chalice up to	*Christ*
Christ, suffering, nailed on	*cross-(1)*
Christ bleeding from hands-(2),	*feet* and gash in chest
angels-(4)	*flying,* one holding chalice up to Christ
Christ bleeding from hands-(2), feet and	*gash* in chest
woman-(1) dressed in black	*gown*
Christ bleeding from	*hands-(2),* feet and gash in chest

CRUCIFIXION

WITH ESTABLISHMENT OF THE CHURCH

(Continued)

angels-(4) flying, one holding *holding* chalice up to Christ

Christ, suffering, *nailed* on cross-(1)

Christ with arms-(2) *outstretched* and bleeding

Christ, *suffering,* nailed on cross-(1)

woman-(1) dressed in black gown

Christ lying on open *casket*

men-(2), loving, placing Christ in *casket*

Christ lying on open casket

Christ wrapped in sheer cloth

men-(2), loving, placing *Christ* in casket

Christ wrapped in sheer *cloth*

Mary *grieving,* touching Christ's hand-(1)

Mary standing silent and *grieving*

Mary grieving and touching Christ's *hand-(1)*

men-(2), *Loving,* placing Christ in casket

Christ *lying* on open casket

women-(2), *man-(1)* and Mary standing

Mary *standing* silent and grieving

women-(2) and *Mary grieving, touching Christ's hand-(1)*

women-(2), man-(1) and *Mary standing*

Mary standing

men-(2), loving, placing Christ in casket

Christ lying on *open casket*

men-(2) placing Christ in *open casket*

men-(2) *placing Christ in open casket*

Christ wrapped in *sheer cloth*

Mary standing *silent and grieving*

women-(2) and Mary *standing*

women-(2), man-(1) and Mary *standing*

Mary *standing silent and grieving*

Mary grieving and *touching Christ's hand-(1)*

women-(2) and Mary standing

women-(2), man-(1) and Mary standing

Christ *wrapped in sheer cloth*

109

Infant Christ clutching *bird-(1)* in hand-(1)

Infant Christ holding *bird-(1)* in hand-(1)

Infant Christ *clutching* bird-(1) in hand-(1)

Infant *Christ* clutching bird-(1) in hand-(1)

Infant *Christ* holding bird-(1) in hand-(1)

Mary wearing *crown*

Mary wearing jeweled *crown*

Infant Christ *holding* bird-(1) in hand-(1)

Mary *holding* Infant Christ in her arm-(1)

Mary *holding* Infant Christ in her lap

Infant Christ clutching bird-(1) in hand-(1)

Infant Christ holding bird-(1) in hand-(1)

Mary wearing *jeweled* crown

Mary holding Infant Christ in her arm-(1)

Mary holding Infant Christ in her lap

Mary sitting on ornate throne

Mary sitting on throne

Mary dressed in *ornate* gown

Mary *sitting* on ornate throne

Mary sitting on *throne*

Context	Keyword
joyous	*angels-(3) playing musical instrument*
	angels-(2) playing musical instrument
Mary lying in	*bed*
Mary lying in straw	*bed*
belt	*belt*
elderly man with pouch and key hanging from	*belt*
Joseph with pouch hanging from	*belt*
Joseph with canteen hanging from	*cane*
Joseph, thoughtful, leaning on	*canteen hanging from belt*
Joseph with	*elderly man with pouch and key hanging from belt*
	grass on ground
	ground
elderly man with pouch and key	*hanging from belt*
Joseph with canteen	*hanging from belt*
Joseph with pouch	*hanging from belt*
angels-(3) playing musical	*instrument*
joyous angels-(2) playing musical	*instrument*
	Joseph, thoughtful, leaning on cane
	Joseph with canteen hanging from belt

111

(Continued)

Joseph with pouch hanging from belt
joyous angels-(2) playing musical instrument
key hanging from belt
leaning on cane
lying in bed
lying in straw bed
man with pouch and key hanging from belt
Mary lying in bed
Mary lying in straw bed
musical instrument
musical instrument
playing musical instrument
playing musical instrument
pouch and key hanging from belt
pouch hanging from belt
stable
thoughtful, leaning on cane
trees
wooden stable

elderly man with pouch and
Joseph, thoughtful,
Mary
Mary
elderly
angels-(3) playing
joyous angels-(2) playing
angels-(3)
joyous angels-(2)
elderly man with
Joseph with
wooden
Joseph,

4.6 SECONDARY SUBJECT MATTER REPRESENTED IN THE THEMATIC CATALOG

In a study to test and refine the method of compiling a thematic catalog, the thematic catalog was constructed from 49 (or 75 percent) of 65 clusters in context. Iconographers identified the secondary meaning of over three-quarters of the clusters in context presented to them; however, they expressed the following difficulties identifying the secondary meaning of clusters in context:

1. No one theme predominated in the cluster in context; descriptive phrases referred to two or more themes.
2. The cluster in context did not convey enough information to describe any theme.
3. The cluster in context did not describe a theme.

These difficulties prevented iconographers from ascribing secondary meaning to a quarter of the clusters in context presented to them.

The process of creating clusters in context required some clustered elements of primary subject matter to be discarded. The two practices involved—creating clusters in context and iconographers' naming of clusters in context—reduced the number of clusters in context and thereby the number of elements of primary subject matter constituting the catalog.

The catalog lists 109 unique elements of primary subject matter, which were grouped into clusters by automatic cluster analyses. Since the catalog presents descriptive phrases in an alphabetical and keyword-in-context format, 139 unique elements of primary subject matter are listed, representing two-thirds of the full set of 208 elements of primary subject matter submitted to cluster analyses. Table 4.1 summarizes the number of unique objects, expressional qualities, and events contributing to the catalog. These figures do not include the additional elements of primary subject matter constituting the catalog that were generated from the keyword-in-context display. The table also shows that a greater percentage of clustered objects contributed to the catalog than expressional qualities or events.

Table 4.2 records the number of unique elements of primary

Table 4.1
Percentage of Clustered Elements of Preiconographical Descriptions Contributing to the Thematic Catalog

	No. clustered	No. represented in catalog	Percentage of Total per category
Objects	105	70	66
Expressional Qualities	43	11	25
Events	60	28	47
Total	208	109	53

Table 4.2
Number of Unique Descriptors Enumerated in Thematic Catalog per Theme

	Adoration of Magi	Agony in Garden	Annunciation	Christ as Man of Sorrows	Crucifixion	Death of Virgin	Entombment	Madonna and Child	Nativity	Resurrection	Total
Number of Unique Descriptors Enumerated in catalog per theme	12	16	40	10	74	11	17	11	22	11	224

Total no. of unique descriptors enumerated in catalog= 139

subject matter enumerated in the catalog per theme. Two themes, "Crucifixion" and "Annunciation," enumerate especially large percentages of the total number of elements of primary subject matter included in the catalog (53 percent and 29 percent, respectively) in comparison to the percentages enumerated in eight other themes represented. This may be attributed in part to the large number of Crucifixions and Annunciations in the full set of 100 works of art used in this study. Many artworks depicted the secondary theme "Madonna and Child" but few unique elements of primary subject matter enumerated in that theme in the catalog. Most likely, these elements were subsumed by the themes "Nativity " and "Adoration of the Magi," in which the Madonna and Child are depicted but appear with other elements, such as St. Joseph or the three wise men.

Interestingly, these 10 themes contain 224 elements. Since there are only 139 unique elements of primary subject matter, 85 elements are contained in at least two themes. Dividing the total number of unique elements enumerated in the catalog per theme (224) by the total number of unique elements enumerated in the thematic catalog (139) produces a measure of overlap. Roughly every other unique element of primary subject matter was enumerated in two themes. Stated another way, the amount of overlap among themes was 62 percent.

Some interesting examples are the "*men-(2)* tied to crosses-(2)" in the theme "Crucifixion" (the good and bad thieves) and the "*men- (2)* placing Christ in open casket" in the theme of "Entombment" (Joseph of Arimathea and Nicodemus). "Mary" appears in the themes of "Adoration of the Magi," "Annunciation," "Crucifixion," "Death of the Virgin," "Entombment," "Madonna and Child," and "Nativity." Instances of overlap are too numerous to mention, but the results of this study clearly indicate that overlapping cluster analysis is required to develop a thematic catalog of primary and secondary subject matter.

Table 4.3 lists iconographers' descriptive names of the secondary themes represented by the 100 artworks and the number of artworks bearing the secondary theme. The entire catalog contains 10 of the 16 groups listed in the table. The following themes are not included: "Ascension," "Pentecost," "Presentation in the Temple," "Visitation," "Saints Groups," and "Por-

Table 4.3
Secondary Subject Matter of Study Artworks

Name	Total No. of artworks	Artwork No. (corresponding to Appendix A for Artworks 1-20)
Adoration of the Magi	4	43, 66, 73, 94
Agony in the Garden	4	8, 45, 67, 78
Annunciation	10	1, 10, 17, 20, 30, 42, 56, 85, 89, 92
Ascension	3	26, 62, 99
Crucifixion	15	4, 11, 19, 24, 27, 37, 48, 55, 61, 70, 80, 84, 88, 93, 97
Death of the Virgin	5	50, 58, 69, 81, 90
Entombment	2	6, 13
Madonna and Child	14	5, 9, 16, 25, 34, 36, 63, 75, 77, 82, 87, 91, 98, 100
Man of Sorrows	3	2, 46, 96
Nativity	5	3, 54, 60, 71, 83
Pentecost	2	35, 86
Presentation in the Temple	3	21, 53, 65
Resurrection	3	12, 15, 51
Saints Groups	2	68, 76
Saints Portraits	2	31, 44
Visitation	2	18, 41
Miscellaneous Scenes	21	7, 14, 22, 23, 28, 29, 32, 33, 38, 39, 40, 47, 49, 52, 57, 59, 64, 72, 74, 79, 95

traits." Typically two or three artworks bear these secondary
themes. There are instances in which the catalog contains a
theme represented by only two or three artworks of the total set
of 100, such as "Entombment," "Man of Sorrows," and "Resurrection," but the small number of artworks representing the
theme may in part explain why the theme is not included in the
catalog. It may also be that these six secondary themes are not
included in the catalog because there are few matching elements
of primary subject matter in artworks depicting the same theme.

When creating clusters in context, a log of artworks whose
composite descriptions contribute descriptive phrases to clusters
in context should be maintained. After clusters in context are
chosen for inclusion in the catalog, descriptions of artworks contributing to the catalog could be discarded. Descriptions of artworks that do not contribute to the catalog should be kept and
submitted to subsequent cluster analyses. In this way, the catalog
is viewed as a dynamic tool, for new entries generated from
subsequent cluster analyses and additions to existing entries can
be made. The thematic catalog described in this chapter is but
one version of a dynamic and changing tool. Artworks whose
descriptions of primary subject matter did not contribute to the
existing catalog should be kept and combined with descriptions
of primary subject matter in newly selected artworks in later
cluster analyses. The process of compiling the thematic catalog
would be repeated and the existing catalog maintained and
updated.

5   Present Methods and Future
         Directions

5.1 METHODS OF SUBJECT ACCESS

This chapter summarizes the methods now in use to describe subject matter in visual resources collections and the indexing approaches applied to the various methods of describing subject matter. As such, it places preiconographical description and the thematic catalog of primary and secondary subject matter into the larger context of methods of subject access to visual resources. The chapter concludes with a discussion of how primary subject matter can be used to improve access to existing visual resources collections and serve as the foundation for constructing a searching tool to enable searchers to consult a visual resources collection without having specialized training in the secondary subject matter upon which the collection is organized and described.

5.1.1 Classification Schemes

When classification schemes are applied to visual resources collections, a systematic or logical arrangement of the collection according to some distinct and useful organizing principle results. The best-known classification scheme whose underlying principle is the secondary subject matter depicted in works of art is Iconclass, developed at the University of Leiden in the

Netherlands by the late Henri van de Waal and Leendert D. Couprie (Couprie, 1978a, 1978b, 1983, 1984a, 1984b; Waal, 1974). Iconclass is a hierarchical classification that places images depicting related themes in proximity to other images depicting such themes. For example, an image depicting prostitution is given Iconclass number 33 C 5; an image depicting a brothel is given Iconclass number 33 C 51; and a man being robbed in a brothel is given Iconclass number 33 C 51 1. When these images are filed into the collection, they are placed in close proximity to one another. Thus, representations of prostitution are in the same filing neighborhood. Browsing for secondary subject matter in a collection organized by Iconclass is facilitated because images sharing common subject matter are together in the same section. The visual resources collection usually associated with Iconclass is DIAL (Decimal Index to Art in the Low Countries), a subscription-based publication in the form of postcard-sized photocards of fifteenth- to seventeenth-century Dutch art. DIAL photocards are arranged in Iconclass number order, which means that images depicting similar secondary subject matter are filed near one another.

Although classification schemes provide a logical arrangement of materials, users of a classified collection have to become familiar with the organizational structure of the scheme. Users of a collection with Iconclass numbers must first translate their secondary subject matter into the appropriate Iconclass number and then search the picture file. An alphabetical index to Iconclass numbers is available to simplify this task.

A number of Dutch institutions use Iconclass to provide access to the secondary subject matter in photographs, printed reproductions, prints, illustrated books, and bibliographies (Couprie, 1983). The Historic New Orleans Collection (THNOC), a collection of historically significant photographs (Sarasan, 1984), and the photographic archive of the Witt Library in the Courtauld Institute of Art (Sunderland, 1983) have announced their intention to use Iconclass in conjunction with computer technology. The Bildarchiv Foto Marburger has introduced a computer-based data entry and retrieval system to access empirical data (artist, height and width of artwork, medium and other categories) and secondary subject matter of 30,000 photographs in the Marburger Index (Heusinger, 1984; K. G. Saur Incorporated, 1983). The machine-readable Marburger Index records include the Iconclass numbers and their English-language caption from the printed and published Iconclass schedules.

Classification schemes have facilitated access to slide collections. The keepers of these collections have identified the important facets common to a large proportion of the collection (chronology, secondary subject matter, medium, geographical area of the artist or photographer, style and so forth) and have expressed these facets in the notation of the class number. When slides are filed in drawers according to class numbers, images on slides that were produced in the same time periods, geographical regions, or stylistic periods are filed in proximity to one another. Thus the slide collection is organized along principles that render the collection a "self-indexing file arrangement" (Irvine, 1979). Although secondary subject matter is often expressed in the class number, the expression of subject matter in the number is usually embedded in the number after alphabetical and/or numerical characters indicating the artist's or producer's name. Thus slides representing the same secondary subject matter as treated by a particular artist are brought together in the same portion of the slide drawer. Class numbers and empirical information on slide labels have been entered into machine-readable form at a number of institutions. Such machine-readable data have typically been sorted by various combinations of facets expressed in the class number, such as chronology-subject-medium and subject-style-medium (Irvine, 1979; Simons and Tansey, 1970). This computer-based sorting of the facets expressed in classification numbers has provided access to the secondary subject matter in slide collections.

Access to secondary subject matter is the underlying principle of Stanford Green's (1981) hierarchical classification for slides and photographs. Green's classification recognizes the needs of amateur photographers and librarians of public library picture collections to organize their collections by broad classification categories that describe general themes (flowers, vacation in Rio, and so on).

Classification schemes employed by keepers of visual resources collections (as well as classification schemes for printed materials such as books and periodicals) have a number of drawbacks:

1. Classification schemes provide a systematic arrangement to the collection that requires the user to know and be familiar with the systematic arrangement. Alphabetical indexes to the classification, such as the one provided by Iconclass, relieve some of the user's burden; however, consulting an index to a classification scheme introduces an additional step to the user's process of searching, which may not be as direct as consulting a single source such as subject headings, and increases the user's chance of making an error.

2. Classification schemes (and their accompanying alphabetical indexes) are controlled vocabularies. Users have to match their terminology, whether the term is a classification code or a term from the alphabetical index, with the term in the scheme to satisfy their needs. A system of cross-references in both the systematic portion and alphabetical index can make it easier for the user to determine the right term or code to use.

3. Classification schemes place the image in one place in the file. Users with little perseverance may not bother to check more than one area in the file and therefore run the risk of missing relevant images. Iconclass rules allow multiple classification codes to be assigned. Multiple codes can be a solution to this drawback in an automated retrieval system of Iconclass numbers and applications such as the Marburger Index.

4. Classification schemes are represented by a classification code of letters and/or numbers and/or symbols. Unless users know the code of interest, they have to consult an alphabetical index to the classification to translate their subject into the classification code and then search the classified file of codes and/or visual images. One solution to this problem is the translation of the classification code into its English-language equivalent as in the online Marburger Index (Heusinger, 1984).

Classification schemes typically provide access to secondary subject matter in visual images. Indexing and browsing techniques applied to classification are explored in section 5.2.

5.1.2 Subject Headings

The use of subject headings has been the most popular approach to identifying subject matter in visual resource collections. For the most part, subject headings have been used to represent secondary subject matter in visual images, but not all subject headings are constructed in the same way. The three most prevalent types are alphabetical lists of subject headings, alphabetico-classed lists of subject headings, and classified lists of subject headings.

Alphabetical lists of subject headings are lists of words or phrases arranged in an alphabetical sequence in a file or catalog. Such lists place the burden of gathering all material on users of the file because they must match terminology with the many subject headings alphabetized in different places in the catalog that treat a particular topic. In a research project to design a prototype retrieval system for multidisciplinary access, Robert Diamond (1969; 1972) developed a list of identifiers (or subject headings) to describe the secondary subject matter in seventeenth-century Western European art. No cross-references from unauthorized to authorized subject headings were given in Diamond's list of identifiers, and no assistance was provided to users interested in subject headings related to other headings, such as *see also* references or broader and narrower headings. Thus a user interested in finding the representations of prostitution had to consult the catalog under many subject headings used to represent the theme of prostitution: "Prostitution," "Brothel," "Courtesan," "Pimps," and others. The inclusion of related terms for *prostitution* in a list of alphabetical subject headings could help users find relevant material. Diamond's work was short-lived because it was a sponsored research project; however, his use of an alphabetical list of subject headings demonstrates the potential difficulties encountered by users of a catalog accessible by alphabetical lists of subject headings.

Subdivisions to main subject headings are also used to describe secondary subject matter. In a catalog comprised of alphabetical headings, there is a main subject heading to which is concatenated one or more subject subdivisions that describe an aspect or specific aspect of the main subject heading. For example, the subject heading "Martin of Tours" may be broken down by subdivisions to represent an aspect of or more specific aspect of the main heading "Martin of Tours" as follows:

Martin of Tours—Celebrating Mass.
Martin of Tours—Dividing his cloak.
Martin of Tours—Meeting devil.
Martin of Tours—Raising hanged man.

Subdivisions of the main subject heading "Martin of Tours" such as "Celebrating Mass" and "Meeting devil" bring together themes that a user might want to select when accessing material on Martin of Tours. The overall arrangement of a catalog employing an alphabetical list of subject headings is an alphabetical arrangement of subject headings; however, subdivisions of subject headings ensure that material depicting specific themes is found in the same filing area of the general theme. In this way, the subdivisions bring together related material, much like a classification scheme brings together related material in a catalog. Thus the subdivisions in an alphabetical list of subject headings are a means of carrying over one of the benefits of a catalog arranged by a classification scheme: bringing together related subjects in a visual resources collection.

There are many lists of alphabetical subject headings used to provide access to secondary subject matter; we will cover only the most important ones as examples. The Index of Christian Art at Princeton University, begun in 1917 by Charles Rufus Morey, now provides access to over 100,000 photographs of medieval art from A.D. 700 to 1400 (Woodruff, 1942, 2). The objectives of the index are

to catalogue by subject and "picture-type" all of the known (published) monuments of Christian art dated before the year 1400, to record briefly the history of the objects, to assemble the important bibliography relating to each monument, and ... to maintain the catalogue by adding to it yearly all of the newly published material and all the pertinent bibliographical references.

The Index of Christian Art is organized along iconographical principles so that subject headings refer to secondary subject matter. Subject headings are actually embedded in prose descriptions of secondary subject matter; however, the index is a card file and is only accessible manually. Consequently subject headings are extracted from the prose descriptions and are listed at the top of cards and filed in alphabetical order in a subject card catalog. One unique subject index to the Index of Christian Art is the Bible Passage index, which lists chapters and verses of the King James edition of the Bible and the corresponding subject headings and subdivisions used in the index to describe the chapter and verse. For example, images depicting "John, xix" are found in the index under "Christ: Flagellation" (verse 1), "Christ: crowned with thorns" (verses 2–3), "Christ: Ecce Homo" (verses 4–7), and so on. The subject headings and subdivisions used to describe secondary subject matter in the Index of Christian Art are used only at Princeton because the subject heading and Bible passage authority files (all authorized headings and cross-references) have never been published or shared with other keepers of visual resource collections. Ohlgren (1978) criticized the Index of Christian Art for its failure to enhance the availability of its subject heading authority file. Subsequently he reported that he obtained a copy of the Index to Christian Art heading list to assist him in the preparation of indexes and descriptions to the secondary subject matter in Anglo-Saxon manuscripts (Ohlgren, 1984).

   The Prints and Photographs Division (P&P) of the Library of Congress maintains a visual arts collection in a variety of formats, including original photographs, prints, cartoons, drawings, posters, and architectural drawings and designs. Betz (1980) compiled a draft list of subject headings to describe the origin, nature, context, and content of the diverse P&P collections. The list is being updated and revised to conform to current thesaurus standards, incorporating the use of direct headings and *bt* ("broader term"), *rt* ("related term"), and *uf* ("used for") references. The inclusion of broader and narrower terms for listed subject headings assists users in gathering all pertinent subject headings on a topic and, eventually, visual images depicting the subjects. P&P staff will use the automatic thesaurus maintenance package LEXICO to help clean up the draft list of alphabetico-classed subject headings. LEXICO will eventually enable Library of Congress patrons to search the subject headings through a computer and enable P&P staff to compile completed lists for distribution to the general public.

   The subject headings list used in the Picture Collection of the

Newark (New Jersey) Public Library is also characteristic of an alphabetical list (Dane, 1968). The basic philosophy of the Picture Collection is to group small and fragmentary topics under main subject headings. As the collection of pictures under a particular main subject heading grows, subdivisions are applied to the main heading. For the most part, pictures are unique and are filed under only one heading in the collection. Consequently subject headings describe the overall theme of a picture and as such treat secondary subject matter. There are other alphabetical lists of subject headings used in or suggested for picture collections in public libraries (Ireland, 1952; Potter and Barton, 1970; Hill, 1975).

Since the mid–1970s, the keepers of visual resources collections have preferred to construct alphabetico-classed lists of subject headings to describe secondary subject matter in visual resources collections. These lists have a foundation of 50 or fewer main subject headings that describe very general topical areas. The subject cataloger then chooses from a long list of secondary headings that describes a more specific aspect of the main heading and concatenates the secondary heading to the main heading. A third heading can be concatenated to the main and second heading; it is the most specific of the three headings.

The *Subject Term Guide* of the National Museum of American Art (NMAA) (1983) consists of 41 main headings; examples are "Abstract," "Allegory," "Animal," "Architecture," "Cartoon," and "Ceremony." Sixteen subject headings listed in the guide can be concatenated to the main heading, but in some instances headings that can be constructed at the second level are suggested rather than prescribed. Headings on the third level are usually constructed by following the guidelines in the guide. Some headings constructed by following the instructions in the guide are: "Animal: Dog: Collie"; "Animal: Bird: Robin"; "Architecture: Castle: Drottningholm Castle"; and "Architecture: Commercial: Skylon Tower." The museum uses the guide to describe secondary subject matter in its permanent collection, the Smithsonian Art Index of art objects in nonart museums of the Smithsonian Institution, the Inventory of American Paintings Executed before 1914, the Pre–1877 Art Exhibition Catalogue Index, the slide and photograph archives, and the Peter

A. Juley and Son Photograph/Negative Collection (Fink and Yarnall, 1984; Allen, 1984).

The Picture Division of the Public Archives of Canada (PAC) had the opportunity to become a contributing member in a nationwide computer network for visual resource collections (National Inventory Programme), but it had little documentation about its collection that could be immediately converted to machine-readable form (Schoenherr, 1981). It has since begun to compile a classified list of subject headings, Thesaurus of Iconographic Terms, to describe its collection of about 100,000 paintings, drawings, watercolors, prints, and posters (Vezina, 1980-1981, 1981). Similar to NMAA's Subject Term Guide, this thesaurus is a classified list of subject headings (Castonguay, 1980, 1981).

The Yale Center for British Art entered empirical data and secondary subject matter into machine-readable form to produce hard-copy indexes to artists, collections, and subjects through the GRIPHOS computer program of the Museum Computer Network (Logan, 1978; Sobinski-Smith, 1980). In 1980, the Yale Center converted its database of 29,000 cataloging records to FOCUS, a database management and online retrieval system (Logan, 1982). FOCUS also manages the center's controlled vocabulary for describing subject matter in artworks (Yale Center for British Art, 1979), which the center compiled to provide subject access to the secondary subject matter in the photographic collection. In the Yale Center's Subject Authority, there are 38 main subject headings for general topics like agriculture, animals, architecture, and caricature. For greater specificity, each main heading can be concatenated by one or two more specific headings. Logan (1982) estimates that there are about 400 subject headings that can be added to main headings and as many tertiary headings.

Alphabetico-classed lists of subject headings may have been inspired by a comparable list devised for the decorative arts collection of the Victoria and Albert Museum. Applied to prints and engravings, the subject headings direct users to prose descriptions that are a combination of primary or secondary subject matter in visual images (Glass, 1969).

Alphabetical lists and alphabetico-classed lists of subject headings typically describe secondary subject matter in visual images. Subject headings answer users' questions quickly. Unlike classification schemes, whose systematic arrangement must be learned by users, subject headings are arranged in alphabetical order in a catalog. Users merely consult the catalog at the appropriate alphabetical location and search for the subject heading of interest. If a subject heading is not listed, users often try a synonym and check another alphabetical location. Some catalogs provide assistance to users, such as cross-references from unauthorized to authorized subject headings, and suggest subject headings that are broader or narrower than the subject heading consulted. Lists of subject headings with such assistance are considered as having a syndetic structure. Subdivisions appended to main subject headings are characteristic of alphabetico-classed lists; such subdivisions ensure that specific aspects of a general subject are found in the same filing area of the catalog rather than dispersed throughout the catalog owing to an alphabetical arrangement. The lists of subject headings have drawbacks, however.

First, alphabetical and alphabetico-classed lists of subject headings separate related subjects and more general subjects than the one consulted. The arrangement of the catalog expects the user to discover related and general subject headings by his knowledge of the subject. Including cross-references and designating broader, related, and narrower relationships between headings partially solve the problem of dispersion. Second, all types of subject heading lists are controlled vocabularies. Users have to match their terminology with the listed subject heading to satisfy their needs. A system of cross-references can help users to arrive at the right term. Searchers also understand subject heading lists more easily than classification codes or numbers because of their verbal construction. Third, a classified list of subject headings resembles a classification scheme in that there is a systematic arrangement to the headings that users must know and be familiar with in order to satisfy their needs. Cross-references in the classified list may help users who proceed down unfruitful paths to find the right search path. In contrast, alphabetical and alphabetico-classed lists of subject headings feature directness of access. If a searcher finds the right subject heading in the catalog, there may be no need to consult another heading to satisfy the inquiry. Finally, classified lists of subject headings do not necessarily list every subject heading in the catalog but make suggestions to the cataloger regarding the construction of a classified subject heading. One solution is for users to check all subject headings at the second level of the full classified subject heading to find pertinent subject heading(s) to express their needs; however, a main subject heading expanded by many tertiary headings could result in a lengthy search.

5.1.3 Prose Descriptions

Prose descriptions have described either primary or secondary subject matter in visual resources collections. In collections developed prior to computerized information retrieval, it was virtually impossible to provide access to every word or phrase in the description, so another method, classification or subject headings, worked alongside the description of subject matter to enable users to find descriptions and visual images matching their subject of interest.

The Index of Christian Art at Princeton University is an example of a visual resources collection employing alphabetico-classed subject headings. In fact, its subject headings are generated from prose descriptions of the secondary subject matter of a visual image. An example (a description for an altarpiece) follows:

Det. center, within architectural frame, Martin, name inscribed, nimbed, mitered, wearing bishop's vestments, holding crozier, seated on bench; sides, 1) Martin of Tours dividing cloak—nimbed beggar grasping cloak cut by Martin, name inscribed, mounted, holding sword: 2–4) Martin of Tours, Scenes—(2) (Raising hanged man, and raising catechumen; greatly destr.)—Martin nimbed, men in bed, one grasped by Martin; men; 2) Virgin Mary nimbed, crowned, seated on bench, suckling Christ Child. 3) (Celebrating Mass)—clergy 2, one with candle; Martin, name inscribed, mitered, wearing pallium, before draped altar on which is chalice; Hand of God issuing arc of heaven. 4) (Meeting devil)—devil beside Martin nimbed, lying in bed; figure. Backgrounds decorated (stucco).

This description of the secondary subject matter in this altarpiece depicting scenes from the life of Martin of Tours is very detailed. Access to every word or phrase in the description would entail much work generating cards and filing them in alphabetical order. Instead, themes of significance are represented by subject headings. In this example, cards bearing subject headings and a reference to the full prose description were most likely constructed for secondary themes, such as "Martin of Tours–Dividing Cloak," "Martin of Tours–Raising Hanging Man," "Virgin Mary–Nimbed," "Martin of Tours–Celebrating Mass," "Hand of God," and "Martin of Tours–Meeting Devil." A user of this index would first consult the subject heading catalog to find subject headings that describe the secondary subject matter of interest and then consult the catalog of full descriptions to filter out unwanted material. Or the user might first consult the subject heading catalog and then proceed directly to the catalog of visual images to select images containing the desired subject matter.

The Frick Art Reference Library's photograph collection numbers nearly a half-million photographs. On the reverse of every photograph mount is a description of the secondary subject matter in the image. A Gilbert Stuart portrait of George Washington is described as follows (Knox, 1979, plate VI):

"Washington, seen against a green curtain, wears a white neckband, a white jabot, and a brownish-red velvet coat and vest with gilt buttons. His eyes are blue, his complexion is ruddy. Some powder from his hair whitens his collar." At lower right, (b) are a landscape, (a) and smoky pink clouds drifting across a blue sky.

Like the Index to Christian Art, access to Frick Art Reference Library photographs and descriptions is provided by an alphabetical catalog to subject headings. The Frick's subject catalog is in card form, which prohibits access to every word or phrase in descriptions of subject matter.

When Ohlgren and Lelvis (1973, 150) compiled a computer-generated index to selected illuminated manuscripts in microform copies of the original holdings in the Bodleian Library, they relied on handlists "compiled over a long period of time by many different hands" to describe the secondary subject matter in the manuscripts. One example of such subject matter descriptions, which formed the basis for a computer-generated subject index, follows (Ohlgren and Lelvis, 1973, 151):

The opening of the seventh seal. Above, God encircled by rainbow. Angel swings golden censer over altar with fire on it. Right, seven angels with seven trumpets. The angel with censer fills it with fire and casts thunders, lightnings, and earthquakes. People try to escape.

Ohlgren selected significant words and phrases from such descriptions, such as *seventh seal, trumpets, angel,* and *God,* to compile a computer-produced index. The index was eventually published as a book, a format that prohibits access to every word or phrase in the description.

This discussion of subject access to visual resources collections has focused on methods of describing subject matter. For the most part, classification schemes, subject headings, and prose descriptions describe secondary subject matter in visual resources collections. Descriptions of primary subject matter have been advocated to provide subject access to these collections so that they can be searched by users who are not equipped with the knowledge and specialized training required to search by secondary subject matter. Primary subject matter is best described by a prose description, such as this example describing the creation of Eve in the St. Peter Altarpiece of Meister Bertram:

God, pointing 2 fingers, haloed, all-knowing, intent, forming Eve with one hand. Adam, naked, sleeping on jagged-ground; Eve, naked, happy, with 2 arms upraised. 2 joyous angels playing musical instrument. Trees in scene.

Throughout this book we have recommended descriptions of primary subject matter such as this example. Primary subject matter can help searchers of a specialized collection of visual images access that collection, without requiring them to be experts in the specialized area that the collection illustrates and upon which it is organized and described. It enhances access to the subject contents of visual images to complement traditional approaches to describing subject content, which have been constrained by the available technology, such as precoordinate indexing and manual file storage, for storage and retrieval. And it offers a method of describing visual images for observers who lack advanced training in the specialized area of the collection. Specialized training is not necessary for indexers who formulate descriptions of primary subject matter.

Sarasan (1984, 392) advocates preiconographical descriptions of visual images for three reasons:

(1) considerable time is saved in the cataloging process since a simple, non-interpretive description is entered rather than a categorization or classification of each work which requires a relatively greater amount of time to assign; (2) a visual description of a work allows a user to envision the composition of the work whereas breaking the visual description into keywords and hierarchies does not; and (3) more visual details may be included in a brief description than can be accommodated by any of the other approaches ... [to] provide the user with a mental image of the work to assist him in judging its relevance to his research.

Sarasan will employ preiconographical description to describe the primary subject matter in a project involving the Historic New Orleans Collection (THNOC) of photographs, prints, and paintings relating to the history of New Orleans.

In yet another example, a database developed by the Interpol Branch of the Canadian Royal Mounted Police in Ottawa contains descriptions of the primary subject matter in stolen works of art (Vance, 1984). The database, RoSA (Repository of Stolen Artifacts), will eventually be available for online subject searching and retrieval through the nationwide Canadian Heritage Information Network. Descriptions of the primary subject matter of stolen artifacts will comprise the database, which will be searched by Canadian police to match recovered artifacts with their legal owners. It is doubtful that such searchers will have specialized training to identify secondary subject matter in historical artifacts correctly. Thus in this application, the decision to describe primary subject matter was a practical one in view of the background and training of the end users of the database.

Descriptions of primary subject matter can be used to generate a thematic catalog of primary and secondary subject matter. Such a catalog opens access to visual resources collections, which have been traditionally described for their secondary subject matter. Consulting the catalog, searchers can translate their query, expressed in primary subject matter, into secondary subject matter and then search the visual resources collection at hand. Thus a thematic catalog of primary and secondary subject matter aids searchers, especially those not having specialized training, to approach a visual resources collection in a preiconographical mode while maintaining the iconographical approach for subject specialists who have been the chief users of many existing visual resources collections.

The thematic catalog examined in this book was produced from a study of 100 late medieval Northern European works of art and organized in a paper format. Primary subject matter is listed in alphabetical order and displayed in a keyword-in-context (or rotated) arrangement. This arrangement is suitable for a paper format in which it is difficult to show each phrase in the context of the entire preiconographical description.

Prose descriptions of subject matter in visual resources collections have three main drawbacks. First, accessing these descriptions has been difficult because of the book or card catalog format employed. A classification scheme or subject headings have had to be instituted in such collections to work in tandem with the description. Second, visual resources collections featuring descriptions of secondary subject matter require exceptional financial support to enable specialized and highly skilled staff to formulate the descriptions. Such support ensures that the search strategies of users knowledgeable of secondary subject matter are maintained. Thus access to primary subject matter in the visual resources collection is not available because the collections' principal users (and the ones providing financial support) do not access the collection in a preiconographical mode. Third, access to primary or secondary subject matter in prose descriptions requires computerized information retrieval to enable direct access to the entire contents of the description. Manual approaches such as book or card catalogs are prohibitively expensive. There are few examples of successful ventures into computerization by visual resources collections (Sarasan and Neuner, 1983), so few organizations have made a commitment to support conversion of catalogs into machine-readable form and computerized information retrieval services. Moreover, few visual resources collections have staff with sufficient knowledge of computerized information retrieval to enable them to make these changes.

The following section explores computerized techniques for indexing and displaying descriptions of both primary and secondary subject matter using each of the three methods of describing subject matter discussed.

5.2 INDEXING AND DISPLAYING OF SUBJECT MATTER

5.2.1 Introduction

To this point, this chapter has presented types of subject matter and methods of subject access. We have covered in depth two types of subject matter (primary and secondary) and the three primary methods that have been applied to the description of primary and secondary subject matter (classification schemes, subject headings, and prose descriptions). What remains is a discussion of indexing and displaying techniques for subject matter of visual resources collections. We will not limit the discussion to indexing and displaying using the existing physical formats of visual resources collections (card, book and paper catalogs) but will extend it to technological advances in optical storage devices and computerized information storage and retrieval.

Four indexing techniques are examined here: phrase indexing, derived search key indexing, keyword-in-context indexing, and keyword indexing. Each technique can be used to access primary or secondary subject matter expressed as a classification code, subject heading, or prose description. Primary subject matter is best expressed in prose descriptions and secondary subject matter in classification codes, subject headings, or prose descriptions. Certain indexing techniques are preferred for certain types of subject matter expressed by a certain method of description. Furthermore, each indexing technique provides possibilities for displaying indexed subject matter in ways helpful to users of visual resources collections.

The three-dimensional matrix in figure 5.1 displays the many possibilities for providing subject access to visual resources collections. At the top of matrix are primary and secondary subject matter, the two types of subject matter suitable for written expression in subject catalogs supporting visual resources collections. On the left side of the matrix are the three principal methods of subject access to visual resources collections. At the bottom of the matrix, the four indexing techniques for visual resources collections are given. The organization of this 2 × 3 × 4 celled matrix seems to indicate that any of the four indexing techniques can be applied to any of the three methods of subject

Figure 5.1
Matrix of Subject Access to Visual Resources Collections

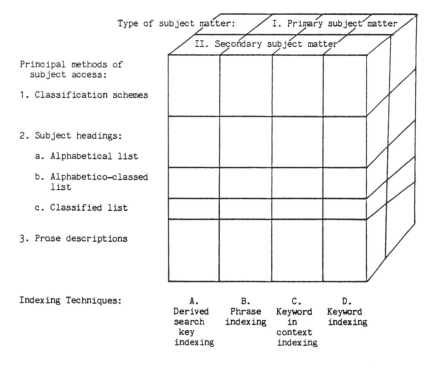

access, or any of the three methods of subject access can be handled by any of the four indexing techniques. In practice, this is not true. Each technique has strengths and weaknesses that make it a strong or weak candidate for application to a particular type of subject matter and method of subject access.

5.2.2 Phrase Indexing

Phrase indexing has been used extensively by keepers of visual resources collections to enable users of these collections to access secondary subject matter. It has been applied to manual, computer-produced, and online subject catalogs. Phrase indexing typically handles subject matter expressed as a subject heading or classification code. Figure 5.2 is an example of an item record for an altarpiece; it contains categories and data for expressing secondary subject matter as a classification code, alphabetico-classed subject headings, and a prose description. Phrase indexing is best suited for the category (or field) called subject heading. In a manual catalog, each listed subject heading is recorded on a card, exactly as it appears in the record, accompanied by the accession number of the item. Subject heading cards are then filed alphabetically in the subject catalog. Thus, a user who looks under the heading "Martin of Tours—Celebrating Mass" would be directed to this full item record (figure 5.2) by the accession number on the subject heading card. Presumably there are other item records that contain the heading "Martin of Tours—Celebrating Mass," and their accession numbers are listed on the subject heading card. Those numbers direct the user to full item records describing the subject matter of other visual images of this theme. In some subject catalogs of visual resources collections, the full item record is given on the subject heading card. This saves time for the user who can proceed directly to the actual visual image without having to spend time on the intermediary step of consulting the catalog of full item records.

The alphabetical arrangement of headings often helps suggest to users themes related to the theme consulted. For example, the hypothetical item record in figure 5.2 lists a number of subject headings beginning with the term Martin of Tours. In an

Figure 5.2
Hypothetical Item Record for an Altarpiece

Accession number: 30 B10 MBArt A,12 A..B

Title of work: Martin of Tours

Medium: Painting

Artist: anonymous

Present location: Barcelona, Museum, Bellas Artes

Format: Altarpiece

Inscriptions: Signature of artist Johannes

Provenance: formerly collection Planduira, Barcelona

ICONCLASS codes: 11 H (Martin), 11 H (Martin) 41, 11 H (Martin) 51

Subject Headings: Martin of Tours---Dividing cloak
                    Martin of Tours
                    Martin of Tours---Raising hanged man
                    Martin of Tours---Raising catechumen
                    Virgin Mary---Nimbed
                    Martin of Tours---Celebrating Mass
                    Hand of God
                    Martin of Tours---Meeting devil

Description: Det. center, within architectural frame, Martin, name inscribed,
               nimbed, mitered, wearing bishop's vestments, holding crozier,
               seated on bench; sides, 1) Martin of Tours dividing cloak -
               nimbed beggar grasping cloak cut by Martin, name inscribed,
               mounted, holding sword: 2-4) Martin of Tours, Scenes -2) (Raising
               hanged man, and raising catechumen; greatly destr.) -Martin
               nimbed, men in bed, one grasped by Martin; men; 2) Virgin Mary
               nimbed, crowned, seated on bench, suckling Christ Child. 3)
               (Celebrating Mass) -clergy 2, one with candle; Martin, name
               inscribed, mitered, wearing pallium, before draped altar on which
               is chalice; Hand of God issuing from arc of heaven. 4) (Meeting
               devil) -devil beside Martin nimbed, lying in bed; figure.
               Backgrounds decorated (stucco).

alphabetically arranged subject catalog, the headings in this item
record create the following subject entries:

Martin of Tours.
Martin of Tours—Celebrating Mass
Martin of Tours—Dividing cloak.
Martin of Tours—Meeting devil.
Martin of Tours—Raising catechumen.
Martin of Tours—Raising hanged man.

A user who consults the heading "Martin of Tours" will probably see the other headings on Martin of Tours when browsing entries in the subject catalog. These headings could inspire the user to narrow the general topic "Martin of Tours" to a specific scene or to check the full item records under each expanded heading to find more material. The alphabetical arrangement of alphabetical or alphabetico-classed subject headings is intended to guide users to other subject headings describing themes related to the theme expressed by the heading consulted.

Phrase indexing is usually applied to classification codes. For example, each Iconclass number in figure 5.2 is indexed exactly the way it appears in the item record and is accompanied by the accession number of the item record. In the case of DIAL (Decimal Index to Art of the Low Countries, 1968), Iconclass numbers are printed on photocards and filed in class number order. Users must know the exact Iconclass number representing the secondary subject matter of their subject of interest. There is an alphabetical index to the Iconclass classification schedules to help users translate their subject of interest into the appropriate Iconclass number(s). Phrase indexing is usually applied to alphabetical indexes of classification schemes and to the classification codes.

For many years, phrase indexing has served keepers and users of visual resources collections. Alphabetical and alphabetico-classed lists of subject headings have been developed by keepers of visual resources collections with the knowledge that these methods exploit the alphabetical arrangement of the subject headings in manual card catalogs by directing users to other relevant subject headings. Consequently phrase indexing is being used in online retrieval systems for visual resources collections with the same good results for users as manual systems.

In an online retrieval system for a visual resources collection, a user types in the subject heading that expresses the secondary subject matter of interest. The online system response is an alphabetically arranged list of subject headings in the alphabetical neighborhood of the user-entered heading. It is also very easy for online systems to maintain a record of the number of times each heading appears in full item records and this information can be displayed. For example, the user interested in Martin of

Tours types this heading into an online information retrieval system for a visual resources collection. The system's response is shown in figure 5.3. The system lists a few subject headings that alphabetically precede the user-entered heading, the subject headings beginning with the user-entered heading "Martin of Tours," and a few subject headings that follow the "Martin of Tours" headings. The online system also lists the number of

Figure 5.3
Hypothetical Online System Response of Phrase Indexing and Display of Subject Headings

```
>User:    Martin of Tours

*System: Check these subject headings in alphabetical order for your entered
         heading.

Line     Subject Headings                              Images

  1      Markets---Yugoslavia---Sarajevo                  1

  2      Markets---Zaire                                  1

 *3      Martin of Tours                                  5

  4      Martin of Tours---Dividing cloak                 4

  5      Martin of Tours---Meeting devil                  1

  6      Martin of Tours---Raising catechumen             1

  7      Martin of Tours---Raising hanged man             2

  8      Masks                                           21

  9      Masks---Burial                                  15

 10      Masks---Ceremonial                               3

OPTIONS:

A.  Browse forward in alphabetical order

B.  Browse backward in alphabetical order

C.  Select line(s) to display information on images

D.  Start over

>User:
```

item records containing the listed heading. It is not enough for the system to reply to the user-entered heading:

MARTIN OF TOURS

5 ITEMS FOUND

An online system should always allow the user to browse forward or backward in the list (see subject headings alphabetically preceding or following the first and last listed heading in the display) and select one or more listed lines to display full item records containing the selected heading(s). Online systems that feature phrase indexing should provide alphabetical lists of headings. After all, the online system has the entire phrase stored; the system only has to place the phrase in the alphabetical neighborhood of other stored phrases. Moreover, users of visual resources collections are accustomed to seeing alphabetical lists of subject headings in manual files and benefit from the alphabetical arrangements of headings by finding other headings in the arrangement to express their subject of interest.

Phrase indexing can also be applied to terms and phrases in the alphabetical indexes to classification schemes. The printed alphabetical index to Iconclass lists significant words and phrases. Under each word or phrase, more complete phrases placing the significant word or phrase in context to an Iconclass theme are listed in classification order according to the Iconclass scheme. Figure 5.4, an excerpt from the printed Iconclass alphabetical index, shows complete phrases listed under the alphabetical index terms *sacrificing* and *sacrilege*. The Iconclass alphabetical index also contains *see also* references that suggest alternative significant words and phrases, which the user can check to find related and/or additional material on listed themes.

In an online alphabetical index to Iconclass, searchers enter their words and phrases of interest; the system then matches user-entered words and phrases with significant words and phrases such as *sacrificing* and *sacrilege*, reports the number of complete phrases listed under the matched significant words, and allows the searchers to browse these complete phrases. Once complete phrases were displayed, the search could be continued in a number of ways: by browsing forward to display complete

Figure 5.4
Iconclass Alphabetical Index

sacrificing

•

•

•

Alexander at the tomb of Achilles; either sacrificing and laying flowers,

or listening to the Iliad being recited 98B (ALEXANDER THE GREAT) 53 8

Augustus closes the gates of the temple of Janus; he may be seen

sacrificing in front of the temple 98B (AUGUSTUS) 56

the courage and piety of C. Fabius Dorsuo (DORSO); dressed in sacerdotal

robes he leaves the Capitol, which was then besieged by the Gauls, to go

and offer a sacrifice on the Quirinal 98 B (FABIUS DORSUO, C.) 51

while Tiberius Gracchus makes a sacrifice two snakes appear (an haruspex

explains the portent; his warning is confirmed soon after, when Tiberius

is killed in an ambush) 98 B (GRACCHUS, TIB. S.) 41 1

death of Themistocles; after making a sacrifice to the gods he drinks

bull's blood 98 B (THEMISTOCLES) 68

Xenophon sacrifices to Diana 98 B (XENOPHON) 51

sacrilege

see also blasphemy

see also desecration

see also profanation

Sacrilege; "Sacrilegio" (Ripa) 11 N 44

•

•

•

phrases following listed phrases, by browsing backward to display complete phrases preceding listed phrases, by selecting a listed complete phrase to obtain information about visual images depicting the theme, or by selecting a listed complete phrase to browse Iconclass headings in the systematic portion of the Iconclass system. Figure 5.5 shows how the complete phrases in the index shown in figure 5.4 could be arranged in an online computerized alphabetical index to Iconclass. One column of information in the online index is not in the printed index: the column labeled "Images" that tells how many visual images depict the theme described by the complete phrase. If the searcher chose option C (select line to display information on images), the system would produce detailed records of the type shown in figure 5.2, composed of the title of the work, medium, location, format, provenance, and accession or filing number of a photograph of the work. Interfacing the online retrieval system and its alphabetical index with an optical disk player and optical disks containing images of indexed visual resources would enable the searcher to obtain the actual visual image of retrieved items at the same work station at which the online search was performed. This frees the searcher from recording accession numbers of retrieved images and manually searching cards, slides, or microforms for photographic reproductions, a practice now necessary when searching visual resource collections such as DIAL, the picture collection of Newark Public Library, or the Index of Christian Art.

If the searcher scanning complete phrases in figure 5.5 had chosen option D (select line to display Iconclass system), the system would have prompted the searcher to select a phrase of interest by entering its line number and then produced the systematic portion of the Iconclass system for the chosen phrase. For example, a searcher might have chosen line 121 on Alexander the Great, and the online system would have listed Iconclass numbers and captions from the Iconclass system. An example of this interaction is shown in figure 5.6, in which the searcher has chosen to see the Iconclass system at "98 B (Alexander the Great) 53 8" by selecting a complete phrase from the online alphabetical index in figure 5.5.

Figure 5.5
Hypothetical Online Alphabetical Iconclass Index

```
>User: Sacrificing

System: Sacrificing (126 complete phrases in index)
```

LINE	ICONCLASS	PHRASE	IMAGES
121	98 B (Alexander the Great) 53 8	Alexander at the tomb of Achilles; either sacrificing and laying flowers, or listening to the Iliad being recited	5
122	98 B (Augustus) 56	Augustus closes the gates of the temple of Janus; he may be seen sacrificing in front of the temple	8
123	98 B (Fabius Dorsuo, C.) 51	the courage and piety of C. Fabius Dorsuo (Dorso): dressed in sacerdotal robes, he leaves the Capitol, which was then beseiged by Gauls, to go to offer a sacrifice on the Quirinal	1
124	98 B (Graccus, Tib. S.) 41 1	while Tiberius Gracchus makes a sacrifice two snakes appear (an haruspex explains the portent; his warning is confirmed soon after, when Tiberius is killed in an ambush)	2
125	98 B (Themistocles) 68	death of Themistocles; after making a sacrifice to the gods he drinks bull's blood	3
126	98 B (Xenophon) 51	Xenophon sacrifices to Diana	1

```
Options:

    A. Browse forward in alphabetical index
    B. Browse backward in alphabetical index
    C. Select line to display information on images
    D. Select line to display Iconclass system
    E. Start over
```

The hypothetical online Iconclass system in figure 5.6 displays captions from the Iconclass system, Iconclass numbers, and the number of images depicting the listed theme. Searchers can browse Iconclass system captions more specific or more general

Figure 5.6
Hypothetical Online Iconclass System

>User: B

System: Enter line number

>User: 121

System: General topic: 98 B (Alexander the Great) 53 other non-aggressive
         activities

LINE	ICONCLASS	DESCRIPTION	IMAGES
1	98 B (...) 53 1	Alexander cuts the Gordian knot with his sword	8
2	98 B (...) 53 2	Alexander has the books of Homer put into a chest	1
3	98 B (...) 53 3	Alexander in his tent, reading works of Homer	2
4	98 B (...) 53 5	Alexander founding Alexandria	17
5	98 B (...) 53 6	Alexander refuses the drink of water offered to him by his soldiers during one of his campaigns	1
6	98 B (...) 53 7	Alexander at the pillaged tomb of Cyrus	1
7	98 B (...) 53 8	Alexander at the tomb of Achilles; either sacrificing and laying flowers, or listening to the Iliad being recited	5
8	98 B (...) 53 9	Alexander as ruler or judge	3

Options:

    A.   Browse more specific descriptions
    B.   Browse more general descriptions
    C.   Select line to display information on images
    D.   Start over

>User:

than listed captions. For example, a searcher wanting to see more general captions than those listed would obtain Iconclass numbers from "98 B (Alexander the Great) 51" to "98 B (Alexander the Great) 59," the corresponding captions to those numbers, and the number of images depicting the themes described by captions. The number of images is a cumulative list of numbers; the number of images for Iconclass number "98 B (Alexander the Great) 53" includes the number of images bearing that exact number and the number of images bearing Iconclass numbers beginning with that number, such as "98 B (Alexander the Great) 53 3" and "98 B (Alexander the Great) 53 92." Iconclass is a hierarchical classification scheme; thus specific numbers for a certain theme are subsumed by general numbers.

Phrase indexing techniques retain most of the drawbacks inherent to the controlled vocabularies (classification schemes and subject headings) to which they are usually applied. When phrase indexing is applied to subject information in machine-readable records of visual images, the resulting computerized retrieval system does little more than the manual system to enhance access to the visual resources collection. But the computerized system does have two obvious advantages over the manual system: it can report the number of visual images depicting a certain theme (as represented by a caption or phrase), and it enables searchers to remain in one place physically, since they do not have to move to a separate drawer of cards or to another index volume while entering words and phrases and matching them with indexed words and phrases.

5.2.3 Derived Search Key Indexing

Derived search key indexing has not been used to index subject information to visual resources collections, but its popularity among automated library catalogs featuring alphabetical lists of subject headings or alphabetical indexes to classification schemes warrants discussion. Derived search keys are usually associated with automated systems; they are built from the first few letters of words in headings. For example, a 5–2–2–1 derived search key for "Martin of Tours—Dividing Cloak" would be "MAR-

TIOFTOD." It contains the first five letters of the first word, the first two letters of the second word, the first two letters of the third word, and the first letter of the fourth word. Keys can be formed by any number of letters.

The major advantage of derived search keys is their ability to save precious and costly storage space in an index file. For example, the search key "MARTIOFTOD" is more compact than the full heading "Martin of Tours— Dividing Cloak" from which it is derived. Searchers who are poor spellers or typists are aided by search keys because they are not required to enter entire words and phrases. Furthermore, derived search keys are formulated by the system based on records entered into the system. Professional staff of the visual resources collection enter the record in figure 5.2 into machine-readable form by typing it into the online system. The system automatically creates derived search keys from data entered into selected categories, such as artist or subject heading categories.

To retrieve records on a particular subject, the searcher re-creates the derived search key for the subject heading of interest and enters it into the system. The system's response is a list of subject headings or derived search keys or individual records matching the user-entered key. Some computerized systems allow searchers to enter the entire subject heading and, without the searcher's knowledge, reformulate the user-entered subject heading into a derived search key.

Derived search key indexing is a type of phrase indexing because it preserves the order of the words within the phrase. When computer storage space is a primary concern, it is an alternative to phrase indexing of subject headings and alphabetical indexes to classification schemes. However, derived search key indexing is not as friendly as phrase indexing because searchers must familiarize themselves with the entry of derived search keys. In a computerized system using phrase indexing, the system can be built to allow searchers to browse the alphabetical index or list of subject headings at whatever alphabetical location they select. The computerized system based on derived search keys requires searchers to match the initial letters in subject headings or alphabetical index terms to browse the file. The latter places a greater burden on the searcher than the former to match entered data (in the required derived search key format) with the controlled vocabulary used to express the subject matter of the visual resources collection. Derived search key indexing is an indexing technique for computerized systems that imposes constraint of indexing technique on the searcher. Thus the searcher is burdened by the limitation of the indexing technique and the drawbacks of the subject heading method of subject access.

5.2.4 Keyword-in-Context Indexing

Keyword-in-context indexing enables searchers to match the innards of a descriptive phrase or subject heading. This type of indexing removes some of the burden from searchers to match their subject inquiries with the one significant word or first word in a descriptive phrase or subject heading under which the phrase or heading is filed. For example, consulting the element of primary subject matter, "hanging," one finds a number of phrases containing this element or term, including the following:

Christ, dead, *hanging* on cross-(1).

Joseph with canteen *hanging* from belt.

In a keyword-in-context arrangement of these descriptive phrases, the term *hanging* is kept in its logical place in the phrase, highlighted and displayed in an alphabetical arrangement that allows the searcher to scan a printed page or display screen quickly to find other terms within the phrase that are relevant to the inquiry. Also, all other terms (except insignificant terms like *a*, *an*, *the*, and *from*) in the phrase are highlighted and displayed in the keyword-in-context arrangement in proper alphabetical order. Thus "Christ," "dead," and "cross-(1)" can be found at the appropriate location in the alphabet. When phrase indexing is applied to the phrase "Christ, dead, hanging, on cross-(1)," the searcher can access only the phrase under the leftmost term, *Christ*. When the same phrase is organized into a keyword-in-context arrangement, the searcher can access the phrase under every significant word: *Christ, dead, hanging,* and *cross-(1)*. Keyword-in-context indexing enhances access to subject information to visual resources by allowing searchers direct access to the inner words of a descriptive phrase or subject heading. Keyword-in-context indexes can be produced manually or by computer. Manual compilation of these indexes is labor-intensive work because every significant word in a subject heading or phrase has to be recorded on paper and filed in its appropriate alphabetical location in a catalog. Provision has to be made for updating the catalog and interfiling new references with previous ones. Thus keyword-in-context indexes have usually been computer produced; updating the catalog entails the production of an entirely new keyword-in-context index in which both new and previously arranged references are manipulated by computer programs. Ohlgren (1977) produced keyword-in-context indexes to descriptive phrases representing the secondary subject matter in medieval manuscripts in the Bodleian Library. The indexes to the manuscripts were produced using a batch computer program and published in a book. Having published the indexes, Ohlgren did not expect to update them; his choice of producing keyword-in-context indexes was a wise one given that periodic updating of the index was unnecessary and that these indexes provided more access points than conventional phrase indexing.

Keyword-in-context indexing provides access to both primary and secondary subject matter and is usually applied to subject headings or descriptive phrases. Besides the limitations already mentioned, searchers of a keyword-in-context index can access only one indexed term at a time. There is no easy way to pinpoint two or more terms of interest contained within a subject heading or phrase in a keyword-in-context index without locating one term of interest and scanning every phrase or subject heading containing the one desired term for the occurrence(s) of the other desired term(s). The only way to access more than one term in a subject heading, classification code, descriptive phrase, or prose description is to apply keyword or component word indexing.

5.2.5   Keyword Indexing

Online computerized information retrieval is the only practical way to provide satisfactory keyword indexing of visual resources' subject matter. Manual alternatives to online computer retrieval are prohibitively expensive because of the personnel resources required to maintain keyword indexing. Keyword indexing of subject matter requires the occurrence of every word in selected categories of an item record to be maintained and stored in a computer index. These occurrence data can be very general or detailed and specific. The degree of detail and specificity recorded by the computer system has a great effect on the system's ability to provide the appropriate information in response to a searcher's inquiry.

A detailed and specific record for keyword indexing requires indexing the following subject information for every significant word in every data category identified as containing subject information (title of work, Iconclass code, subject heading, and description data categories):

1. Item record accession number.
2. Data category.
3. Sentence number within the data category in which the word resides.
4. Word position within the sentence in which the word resides.

When all of these data are processed and stored by the computer, searchers can find:

1. One or more terms that occur in an item record.
2. One or more terms that occur in the same or different data categories in an item record.
3. One or more terms that occur in the same sentence in a data category.
4. One or more terms that occur within the same sentence and within a designated number of terms to one another in a data category as designated by the searcher.

At a minimum, online computerized retrieval systems featuring keyword indexing allow searchers to find one or more terms that occur in an item record, which means that only the term and accession numbers of item records bearing this term are stored in computer indexes. The more data that are stored in computer indexes about sentence order and word position, the more expensive it becomes to maintain, update, and search the indexes. Online searchers, however, can enter specific requests into the computer and retrieve specific and precise results.

Keyword indexing and retrieval has been closely associated with the Boolean operators AND, OR, and NOT because these operators allow searchers to combine the terms of their subject inquiries in special ways. For example, if the subject information in the hypothetical item record in figure 5.2 were indexed as described, a searcher interested in retrieving images assigned the subject heading "Martin of Tours—Celebrating Mass" might use the AND operator and enter the following search statement into a computerized system:

1. FIND DESCRIPTION MARTIN AND TOURS AND MASS

This statement instructs the system to find all item records whose description data category contains the terms *Martin, Tours,* and *Mass.* Venn diagrams have been used to describe how Boolean operators work in online computerized retrieval systems. The shaded portion in figure 5.7 shows the item records retrieved by search statement 1 in which the Boolean AND operator is used. The remainder of the Venn diagram, which is outlined but not shaded, shows item records containing one or two of the desired terms but not all three terms. Presumably the item record in figure 5.2 would be retrieved by the search statement because the record contains all three terms in the description data category. The system's response to the searcher-entered subject information should show the number of item records bearing the entered terms, provide an option to display on the screen full- or short-item records to allow users to determine whether they have found what they want, and provide an option to continue entering additional subject information.

The searcher could also command the computerized retrieval system to find all the items bearing an image of the hand of God. To enter this into the system, the searcher could use the AND operator or an adjacency command that is like the AND operator but is more stringent because the terms entered must occur in the same record, same data category, same sentence, and adjacent one another. In such a search statement, the searcher might enter into the system:

Figure 5.7
Venn Diagram Showing Items Retrieved by Boolean AND Operator

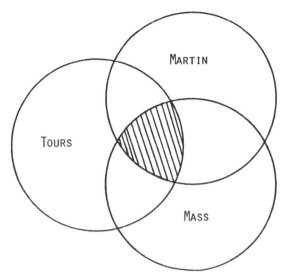

2. FIND HAND ADJACENT GOD
to find items depicting the hand of God. Keyword indexing systems typically report the number of item records bearing the searcher-entered terms and maintain these results while the searcher continues entering inquiries. Consequently the searcher could now find all items depicting both Martin of Tours celebrating Mass and the hand of God by combining the results of search inquiries 1 and 2 using the AND operator. The searcher would find items depicting both images by entering:
3. FIND #1 AND #2
Conversely the searcher might want to see images of Martin of Tours celebrating Mass without the hand of God represented in the scene. The searcher would find items depicting Martin of Tours celebrating Mass but not the hand of God by using the NOT operator:
4. FIND #1 NOT #2
    The shaded portion in the Venn diagram in figure 5.8 shows the item records retrieved by search statement 4 in which the

Figure 5.8
Venn Diagram Showing Items Retrieved by Boolean NOT Operator

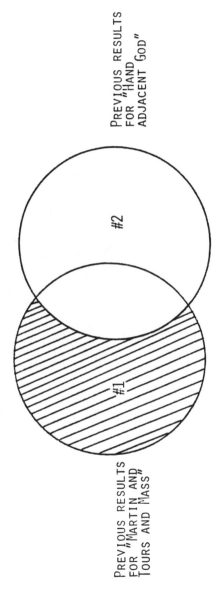

PREVIOUS RESULTS FOR "HAND ADJACENT GOD"

#2

#1

PREVIOUS RESULTS FOR "MARTIN AND TOURS AND MASS"

Boolean NOT operator is used. The remainder of the Venn diagram, which is outlined but not shaded, shows item records containing undesired terms.

At this point, the searcher might choose to display detailed information on a few records to determine whether references to images pertinent to the expressed interest have been retrieved. Perhaps the searcher now wants images of Martin of Tours celebrating Mass in which neither the hand of God nor an altar appears. The searcher would first find all item records bearing the terms *hand of God* and *altar* by relying on the results of request inquiry 2, in which the hand of God was specified and combining those results with another term, *altar*, using the OR operator:

5.   FIND #2 OR ALTAR

The results of search statement 5 contain images depicting the hand of God and images depicting an altar. The shaded portion in figure 5.9 shows item records retrieved by search statement 5 in which the Boolean OR operator is used. In this Venn diagram, both circles are shaded because the searcher eventually wants to retrieve items depicting either the hand of God or an altar to separate these items later from items depicting Martin of Tours celebrating Mass.

Figure 5.9
Venn Diagram Showing Items Retrieved by Boolean OR Operator

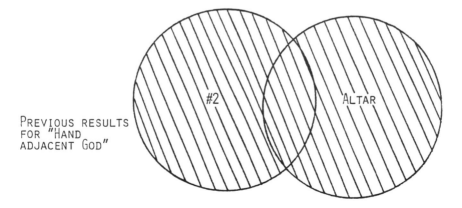

To find items in which no altar or hand of God is depicted, the searcher combines the results of search statement 1 for Martin of Tours celebrating Mass and search statement 5:

6. FIND #1 NOT #5

In response to search statement 6, the system retrieves item records representing images that depict Martin of Tours celebrating Mass in which neither an altar nor the hand of God is depicted. Presumably the item record in figure 5.2 would *not* be retrieved because Martin of Tours is depicted celebrating Mass with two criteria—altar and hand of God—that the searcher does not want represented in the image.

Keyword indexing and retrieval systems are designed according to some general guidelines and resemble one another with respect to:

1. Creation of successively numbered sets in response to the entry of search statements.
2. Availability of Boolean operators AND, OR, and NOT.
3. Recovery of results in previously created sets for use in subsequent search statements.

Little else about keyword indexing and retrieval systems is the same from system to system. With regard to keyword indexing in retrieval systems, no two systems index the same information in the same way, and no two systems have the same user-system interface for retrieving information. The second point is more important because searchers have to learn how to use the online computerized retrieval system to obtain satisfactory results to their queries. When the user-system interface (the computer program that accepts the searcher's requests, expresses them to the system, and communicates the system's response to the request back to the searcher) differs from system to system, searchers must continually learn how to use and master the capabilities of different systems.

The effort involved in implementing an online system with keyword indexing is worthwhile, however, because keyword indexing in online information retrieval systems allows searchers to match their terminology with the indexed contents of data categories containing subject information (classification codes, subject headings, and prose descriptions) regardless of a term's location in a data category (as the first, middle, or last term in a subject heading). Furthermore, these systems allow searchers to enter more than one term into the system and find various logical combinations of terms. No longer is the searcher constrained to finding images bearing a single subject heading or term and then scanning all the retrieved item descriptions or images to find the one(s) that contain another criterion(a).

The various types of subject headings that describe secondary subject matter are considered a *precoordinate* indexing technique because the subject heading is devised during the indexing process, before retrieval takes place. Keyword indexing and retrieval systems are considered a *postcoordinate* indexing technique because the retrieval of item records is based on the searcher's criteria during the retrieval process, after the indexing process. That is not to say that postcoordinate indexing techniques such as keyword indexing cannot be applied to precoordinate indexing techniques. In fact, postcoordinate indexing is often successfully used to enhance retrieval of precoordinate subject vocabularies. However, the opposite—applying precoordinate indexing techniques to terminology such as prose descriptions—is not recommended because the retrieval of subject information must be limited to selected subject-rich words or phrases.

Postcoordinate indexing techniques can be applied to precoordinate indexing vocabularies and lead to fruitful results. Imagine searching the entire Iconclass system and index to find classification areas treating images of caged birds, human sacrifices, or raising-of-the-dead miracles by saints. To perform such searches, the terms in the Iconclass system and index would be entered into keyword indexes; the result of a keyword search for "raising-of-the-dead miracles by saints" would direct searchers to the Iconclass areas where images depicting these miracles would be classed.

Some computerized systems have been used to access subject matter of visual images through keyword indexing and searching techniques. Bisogni (1978) uses the STAIRS information retrieval system to access prose descriptions of the secondary subject matter in Italian works of art. STAIRS is also used to access secondary subject matter descriptions of works of art in the Marburger Index (Heusinger, 1984). Iconclass has been applied to images in the Marburger Index, but retrieval is permitted through both Iconclass numbers and keywords in the text of Iconclass. The Canadian Heritage Information Programme (CHIN) provides the BASIS retrieval system to its members, who use BASIS's keyword and Boolean-based retrieval techniques to access the secondary subject matter of artifacts and artworks in Canadian museums; a CHIN database has also recently been built to help trace stolen works of art. Both primary and secondary subject matter will be identified in this database, which will be searchable using the BASIS retrieval system and its keyword indexing and searching capabilities.

Keyword indexing and retrieval capabilities have been applied to existing visual resources collections to provide access to secondary subject matter because these collections have been accessible only through secondary subject matter over the years. Thus the new technology in computerized information retrieval has been applied to an already existing method of subject access. Computer technology can enhance existing subject access through retrieval of the inner text of subject headings or the logical combination of multiple words or characters in subject headings or classification codes, but the technology cannot provide subject access to much more than what already exists in the item record—that is, secondary subject matter.

5.3 PRIMARY SUBJECT MATTER AND VISUAL RESOURCES COLLECTIONS

Access to the subject matter of visual resources collections has typically been provided through controlled vocabularies such as subject headings and classification schemes that describe secondary subject matter. For a long time, indexes and catalogs to subject matter have been accessed manually by searchers. Controlled vocabulary entries have to be prepared and filed in the index or catalog in their proper place, a costly process. Thus controlled vocabularies were developed to describe the secondary subject matter of a visual image; only one or two controlled vocabulary terms were necessary to describe the image's secondary subject matter. As long as indexes and catalogs were manual tools, secondary subject matter remained the only practical approach to accessing the subject matter of visual resources because primary subject matter required the preparation and filing of multiple entries per image.

Technology now allows us to overcome limitations of manually produced tools such as indexes to and catalogs of secondary subject matter. Indexing of every controlled vocabulary term and logical combinations of terms is easily accomplished by computer. Special keyword-in-context indexes that were prohibitively expensive to compile manually can now be computer prepared for online or offline browsing. Thus the constraints imposed by manual indexing and access techniques have been lifted because computer technology can easily and inexpensively provide multiple access points to a single visual image. Since prose descriptions of primary subject matter are composed of many terms per image, this type of subject access method is a prime candidate for applying computer technology such as keyword indexing, logical combinations of terms through Boolean operations, and/or preparation of special online or computer-produced offline indexes.

This book has focused on the development of a thematic catalog of primary and secondary subject matter. A thematic catalog is meant to aid searchers of visual resources collections who do not have knowledge of secondary subject matter. Such a catalog allows them to translate their primary subject matter into the appropriate secondary subject matter and then search the iconographical research collection at hand. Thus the catalog is constituted of primary and secondary subject matter.

The thematic catalog is a dynamic tool, continually being maintained and updated as new visual images are added to the collection to serve searchers. Primary subject matter descriptions for visual images contributed to the latest version of the catalog would be withdrawn from the computer file. Preiconographical descriptions of artworks that failed to contribute to the thematic catalog would be left in, combined with new artworks in subsequent cluster analyses. In this way, the process of compiling a catalog would be repeated frequently, and updated editions of the catalog could be accessed in printed format through a key-word-in-context display or in an online mode through keyword indexing and retrieval techniques.

Figure 5.10 shows the process of maintaining and updating a thematic catalog of primary and secondary subject matter to an existing visual resources collection in which access to secondary subject matter is already provided. The major changes from the process of compiling a thematic catalog are (1) selection of art-works from an existing visual resources collection (step 1), (2) preparation of composite descriptions of primary subject matter by a single observer (step 2), (3) checking clusters in context with the previously identified secondary meaning of visual images in the collection (step 5A), and (4) saving and discarding unused and used preiconographical descriptions (steps 6A and 6C).

Whenever new editions are produced, the online thematic catalog is updated (see figure 5.10, step 6B). One can envision an online thematic catalog coexisting in an online database of visual images available for searching and retrieval. Verbal descriptions of the images would constitute the database. For example, the description of an artwork illustrating St. Francis receiving the Stigmata is contained in Bisogni's online "Catalogue of Italian Art" and is available for keyword searching in an online database of Italian artworks (figure 5.11). The description enumerates empirical data about the artist, owning institution, date of execution, that is, data in addition to the artwork's secondary subject matter, residing in the description and figure-scene categories. Since the construction of the thematic catalog requires the identification of the visual image's primary subject matter (preiconographical descriptions), accounts of artworks in online databases must be improved to include preiconographical descriptions. Then searchers of online databases of artworks will be able to access the database in either a preiconographical or iconographical mode.

An online thematic catalog can serve as a searcher's tool in the database of artworks. Searching an online thematic catalog differs from searching a printed version of the catalog because it allows keyword retrieval and multiple coordinations of descriptors through the use of Boolean operations AND, OR, and NOT. Searchers could query an online thematic catalog with more than

Figure 5.10
**Flowchart of the Process of Maintaining and Updating a Thematic Catalog
of Primary and Secondary Subject Matter**

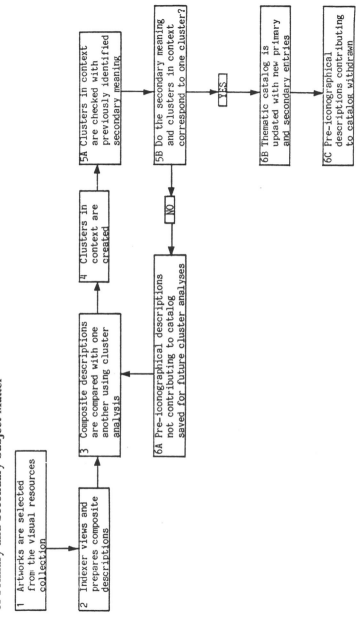

Figure 5.11
Online Database Record in the "Catalogue of Italian Art"

COMPILERS: Fabio Bisogni Laura Corti

PLACE: Boston

PROVINCE: Massachusetts

STATE: USA

LOCATION: Isabella Stewart Gardner Museum

INV-CAT: Inv. F 27 E 46

SCHOOL: Riminese

AUTHOR: Giuliano da Rimini, signed

DATE: 1397

COMMISSION: Confraternita Della Buona Morte

MEDIUM: Tempera on wood. Horizontal rectangular dorsal. Painted as
                  a polyptych subdivided by painted spiral columns ...

RESTORATION: Restored in 1942-44.

INSCRIPTIONS: Signed on the top border: anno domini millennio ccc settino
                  iulianus pictor de arimino decit ochopus (sic!) tempore ...

DESCRIPTION: Central image: Madonna Enthroned with child. Upper
                  register, left side, right image: scene from the life of
                  St. Francis of Assisi (as a devotional image): St. Francis
                  receiving stigmata ...

PROVENANCES: Urbania, Church of San Giovanni Decollato also called Chiesa
                  dei Morti.

BIBLIOGRAPHY: 1974, Hendy, pp. 110-12, pl. 1.

PHOTOS: All photos museum. Entire: B. R. (1925) B130; B. R. (1941)
                  B 921; A. R. (1957) BB1311. Central part: A. R. (1957)
                  B1327. Madonna and Child: B. R. ...

FIGURE-SCENE: ... St. Francis of Assisi receiving stigmata. In a rocky
                  landscape with plants, St. Francis, middle-aged, tonsured,
                  with black hair and short beard, wearing the Franciscan
                  habit and sandals. He kneels on his right knee, his hands
                  half-lifted, receiving stigmata from a seraph-like crucified
                  Christ. L. S.: Celano I, 94-6; Bonaventura XIII, 3. ...

SOURCE: Fabio Bisogni, "The 'Catalogue of Italian Art': A computer-produced
         iconographical analysis," Museum 30 (1978): 203.

one preiconographical descriptor in mind, such as "Christ and holes and bleeding." If such a search were presented to the online thematic catalog, the searcher would obtain two results: the secondary meaning of the phrase (for example, "Crucifixion" or "Man of Sorrows") and a subset of visual images in the online database depicting the "Crucifixion" or "Man of Sorrows." In contrast, a printed version of the thematic catalog allows the searcher to look up elements of the phrase only one at a time and can feature only the first result, the secondary meaning. An example of such an interaction between the searcher and computer system is shown in figure 5.12.

Some embellishments to an online thematic catalog of primary and secondary subject matter also come to mind. The catalog could contain cross-references from a synonym describing a secondary theme, such as "Christ on Mount of Olive," to the preferred term used by the thematic catalog, "Agony in the Garden." Users of one visual resources collection are probably accustomed to the controlled vocabulary used in that collection. Searchers who are familiar with the searching vocabulary of one collection and find themselves accessing a different collection but one specializing in the same subject area are bound to have difficulty matching the controlled vocabulary terms of the second collection. Including alternate ways of expressing the same theme in the thematic catalog confines the searcher's task of translating a query into secondary subject matter to the thematic catalog. Otherwise the searcher would have to consult secondary sources—in the case of iconographical research collections, dictionaries of Christian themes and symbols—to find the accepted term used in the iconographical research collection at hand.

Augmenting the thematic catalog's compilation of secondary subject matter by including synonymous terms for secondary subject matter would entail a separate section in the catalog or integration of these synonymous terms in the secondary subject matter compilation; the latter would require an alphabetical index to accommodate users who approach the secondary subject matter compilation with the synonymous term in mind. In constructing future thematic catalogs, we recommend that the synonymous terms for expressing secondary subject matter be included in the thematic catalog. The thematic catalog could also

Figure 5.12
Hypothetical User-System Interaction in an Online Thematic Catalog and Visual Image Database

```
System:   Enter your query.

User >:   Find Christ bleeding from holes on hands

          A.   Show symbolic descriptions representing this topic
          B.   Show number of images on this topic
          C.   Show images
          D.   Start over


User >:   A

          System:
                For this topic, search also under
                      Crucifixion
                      Man of sorrows
                      Noli me tangere

          A.   Show number of images on this topic
          B.   Show images
          C.   Start over
```

```
User >:   A

          System:   280 images found
                    Options:
                    A.   Show brief verbal descriptions
                    B.   Show images
                    C.   Limit result with another term
                    D.   Start over
```

include Iconclass numbers (Waal, 1974) for secondary subject matter as yet another way of expressing secondary subject matter.

We also recommend that those compiling a thematic catalog limit their choice of visual images to a particular medium, geographical area, and chronological period. Clustering preiconographical descriptions to Etruscan sarcophagi and photographs of everyday American life in the nineteenth and twentieth centuries would not be in keeping with Gombrich's (1972) notion of the dictionary fallacy in which images must be interpreted in the light of their context.

Compilation of a thematic catalog requires selection of visual images that convey secondary meaning. Some visual images do not bear a second level in the study of meaning or subject matter—for example, modern landscapes, still lifes, and nonobjective art (Teyssedre, 1964).

A thematic catalog of primary and secondary subject matter is a searching aid to visual resources collections to enable users to search collections without knowing the secondary meaning of the representational elements in the visual image. The searching aid, a thematic catalog of primary and secondary subject matter, is developed by a process featuring untrained observers' descriptions of the primary subject matter in visual images, automatic grouping techniques, and the identification of secondary meaning by subject specialists.

The thematic catalog can be accessed manually in a printed compilation featuring keyword-in-context indexing. It can also be an online searcher's tool to an online database of primary and secondary subject matter descriptions of visual resources. Computer technology allows searchers to match multifaceted queries (those composed of more than one facet or concept) with the primary or secondary subject matter represented by visual images in the visual resources collection. An online thematic catalog allows searchers to retrieve the number and description of visual images in the database matching their queries and/or to obtain the secondary subject matter represented by the primary subject matter terms they enter.

Descriptions of primary subject matter are now included in an online database of stolen works of art and are proposed for an online database of historical New Orleans photographs. Such descriptions are included in item records that also detail secondary subject matter, but so far compilation of a thematic catalog of primary and subject matter has not been proposed for either database. However, the inclusion of both types of subject matter in item records should enable online searchers entering queries composed of primary subject matter to retrieve item records, check the secondary subject matter in retrieved item records, and enter subsequent queries composed of the secondary subject matter common to the majority of retrieved item records. In this way, searchers could augment their search strategies to find additional relevant items by using the subject information detailed in retrieved, relevant items.

Descriptions of primary subject matter can also serve as intermediary subject representations of visual images and be stored in online databases until a detailed scholarly analysis can be performed by a subject specialist. In this way, the image is accessible to searchers who approach the collection with a resume of representational elements or primary subject matter. In comparison to manually produced and maintained catalogs and indexes, computer technology is a medium that allows inexpensive storage and efficient retrieval of primary subject matter descriptions. Technological advances in image storage such as micrographic formats and optical disks have shown that reproduction and distribution of the visual images far surpass the capability to provide subject access to the stored images. Image databanks such as the Marburger Index (Heusinger, 1984) and Witt Archive (Sunderland, 1983) are composed of hundreds of thousands of visual images; however, subject access to the entire databank lags far behind image availability. Identification of primary subject matter to these images is a viable alternative until the images' secondary subject matter has been identified by subject specialists.

This study on developing a thematic catalog of primary and secondary subject matter in art was exploratory. It was intended to achieve new insights into and gain familiarity with primary subject matter and its associated themes and concepts. The principal objective was to develop the thematic catalog with the aid of computer techniques. The objective was achieved despite the limitations of an exploratory study.

The number of artworks used to compile the catalog in this study was limited to 100; the works were not associated with any particular visual resources collections. Obviously, in practice, thematic catalogs would be constructed as tools to a specific visual resources collection. These thematic catalogs would not only allow searchers to translate their requests expressed as primary subject matter into the proper secondary subject matter but would be a gateway to the visual images in an existing visual resources collection.

It is not difficult to imagine the searcher of the future seated at an image work station in which primary and secondary subject matter descriptions and representations of the visual images themselves are accessible through digital and optical storage and retrieval techniques. The searcher merely enters a single or multifaceted query and retrieves verbal descriptions of subject matter and high-resolution photocopies from optical disks of the retrieved images to use and compare at his own discretion. Such image work stations have already been developed for retrieval of patent information and images. Primary subject matter descriptions and a thematic catalog of primary and secondary subject matter are new, innovative approachs to improving access to the subject matter of visual images, which permit searchers from a variety of disciplines and subject backgrounds to find representations in visual resources collections.

APPENDIX A

Sources of Reproductions and Preiconographical Descriptions for Twenty Works of Art

Twenty works of art used in this study to compile a thematic catalog are listed below along with identifying information—title, artist, date, owning institution, and sources of reproductions—and preiconographical description. A key to the sources follows the list.

1. Annunciation from Vyssi Brod Cycle
Meister von Hohenfurth
c1350–1355
Prague, National Gallery

Seibt, ill. 88

AT, cat. 132, pl. 23

Glaser, pl. 3

Burger, I, tf. X

Stange, I, abb. 176, 177

Matejcek, pl. 4

Musper [GM], pl. 137

MARY-BV, UNATTENTIVE, ALOOF AND HALOED, SITTING ON ORNATE-THRONE WITH CUSHION AND PILLARS-(2), PAGING THRU OPEN-BOOKS-(2). ANGEL-(1), BAREFOOT AND WITH WINGS-(2), KNEELING BEFORE MARY, BECKONING HER WITH OUTSTRETCHED HAND-(1), AND HOLDING ORB-(1) AND BANNER. GOD, DRESSED IN WHITE-GOWN, OBSERVANT AND HALOED, BECKONING WITH OUTSTRETCHED HAND-(1). TREE-(1) AND FLOWER-3-STEMMED IN SCENE.

2. Man of Sorrows Seated against Stem of Cross, Mary and John (Arma Christi)
Master of the Votive Panels of St. Lambert
c1425
Berlin, Staatliche Museum

Stange, XI, abb. 25   Stange [DGM], pl. 76
Schiller, II, pl. 743
CROSS-(1) STANDING-UPRIGHT AND LADDER-7-STEPPED AND
LANCES LEANING AGAINST IT. CHRIST, DEAD, HALOED,
DRESSED IN LOINCLOTH, LEANING AGAINST CROSS NEAR
OPEN-CASKET. MARY-BV, HALOED, PRAYING AND MAN-(1)
WITH CURLY-HAIR AND HALOED SITTING, BOTH GRIEVING
WITH HOPELESSNESS. DARK FIGURE, SUSPICIOUS, STAND-
ING AT GATEWAY TO TOWN. TREES AND BLACKENED-HILLS
IN DISTANCE.

3. Nativity from Altar of St. Peter
Meister Bertram
c1379
Hamburg, Kunsthalle
Glaser [AM], pl. 27   Winkler, abb. 42
Glaser [ZJdM], abb. 21   Stange, II, abb. 167
Musper [GM], pl. 168   Lichtwark, s. 227
Platte, tf. 21   Portmann, tf. 20
MARY-BV, SERENE AND HALOED, SITTING ON CUSHION,
WITH OUTSTRETCHED ARMS-(2) TOWARD CHRIST-AS-IN-
FANT. JOSEPH, INTENT, WITH WHITE-HAIR AND BEARDED,
IS STANDING AND HANDING WITH OUTSTRETCHED HAND-
(1) CHRIST-AS-INFANT, DRESSED IN LOINCLOTH, HALOED,
TO MARY. JOSEPH DRESSED WITH CANTEEN HANGING FROM
BELT. DONKEY, PLEASED, AND GOAT, QUESTIONING, LYING
WITHIN COLLAPSING WOODEN-STABLE. COOKING-POT AND
BASKET NEARBY.

4. Crucifixion from a Diptych
c1330–1335
Cologne, Kaiser Frederick Museum
Burger, II, abb. 449   Stange [DGM], pl. 20
Simson, fig. 274   Reiners, abb. 3
Stange, I, abb. 26
CHRIST HANGING DEAD ON CROSS-(1), DRESSED IN LOIN-
CLOTH, WITH HEAD INCLINED, HALOED, AND WITH OUT-
STRETCHED ARMS-(2), FEET CROSSED AND BLEEDING.
WOMEN-(3) AND MAN-(1) WITH CURLY-HAIR AND UPRAISED
HAND-(1), RESERVED AND BESEECHING, SUPPORTING MARY-
BV. MAN-(1), INTENT AND DRESSED IN CAP, STANDING WITH
ARM-(1) UPRAISED TOWARD BANNER. ANGELS-(2) FLANKING
CROSS-(1).

5. Glatz Madonna
c1350–1355
Berlin, Staatliche Museum
Seibt, ill. 87   Musper [GM], p. 157
Matejcek, pl. 28   Stange [DGM], pl. 11
MARY-BV, SERENE AND REMOVED, DRESSED IN SCARF, OR-
NATE-GOWN, HALOED, SITTING ON ORNATE-THRONE AND
HOLDING ORB-(1), SCEPTRE. CHRIST-AS-INFANT, THOUGHT-
FUL, HALOED, WITH HEAD INCLINED, CLUTCHING AND
STANDING ON LAP OF MARY. MAN-(1) PRAYING AND ADMIR-
ING WITH SWORD NEARBY. CANOPY COVERING WITH SHUT-
TERS-(2) AND CROSSES-(2). LIONS-(2) SQUATTING. ANGEL-(1)
PRAISING WITH ARMS-(2) OUTSTRETCHED, PROTECTIVE.
ANGELS-(2), PASSIVE, SWINGING CENSERS-(2) AND LEANING.
ANGELS-(2), JOYOUS, WITH OUTSTRETCHED ARMS.

6. Entombment from Trebon Altar
c1385–1390
Prague, National Gallery
Seibt, pl. VIII
Stange, II, abb. 66
CHRIST, HALOED, LONG-HAIR, REMOVED, WRAPPED IN
SHEER-CLOTH, DRESSED IN LOINCLOTH, AND LYING IN
OPEN-CASKET. FEET AND HANDS-(2) BLEEDING AS MEN-(2),
LOVING, BOTH BEARDED AND LONG-HAIR AND ONE WITH
CAP, ARE PLACING HIM IN SMOOTH CASKET. WOMEN-(2),
MAN-(1) WITH CURLY-HAIR AND MARY-BV, ALL HALOED,
STANDING, SILENT AND GRIEVING. STONY-GROUND.

7. Veronica with the Sudarium
Meister Wilhelm von Köln
c1410–1420
Munich, Alte Pinakothek
Stange, III, abb. 65   Glaser [ZJdM], abb. 28
Burger, II, tf. XXVII   Winkler, abb. 54
Glaser, pl. 15   Glaser [AM], abb. 33
WOMAN-(1), SILENT AND HALOED, DRESSED IN CAPE, HOLD-
ING IN HANDS-(2) CLOTH WITH CHRIST'S-FACE WHICH IS
MOROSE AND WITH LONGING IN HIS DARK-EYES, AND LONG-
HAIR, BEARDED AND HALOED.

8. Christ on Mt. Olive from Vyssi Brod Cycle
Meister von Hohenfurth

c1350–1355
Prague, National Gallery
Simson, pl. XXX   Burger, I, abb. 145
Matejcek, pl. 10   Stange, I, abb. 176
CHRIST, BAREFOOT, LONG-HAIR, HALOED, DRESSED IN
GOWN, KNEELING ON HILL, BESEECHING WITH HANDS-(2)
OUTSTRETCHED. ANGEL-(1) IN CLOUD-(1) WITH WINGS-(2)
AND HALOED IS OBSERVANT. MEN-(3) SITTING AND SLEEP-
ING ON JAGGED-GROUND, ARMS-(2) FOLDED ON KNEES.
BIRDS-(3) SITTING IN TREES.

9. Madonna Enthroned from Diptych
c1330–1335
Cologne, Kaiser Frederick Museum
Simson, fig. 274   VSL, p. 98
Stange [GP], pl. 35   Stange, I, abb. 25
Stange [DGM], pl. 20   Reiners, abb. 3
MARY-BV, REMOVED, SITTING ON ORNATE-THRONE,
DRESSED IN GOWN AND CROWN, HOLDING FLOWER-3-
STEMMED AND CHRIST-AS-INFANT ON LAP, WHO IS STAND-
ING, HALOED, BAREFOOT, DRESSED IN GOWN, AND WITH
CURLY-HAIR, AND TOUCHING CHEST AND CHIN OF MARY
WITH HIS HAND-(1).

10. Annunciation
c1320
Cologne, Wallraf-Richartz
Stange [GP], pl. 35   Reiners, abb. 1, pl. II
Stange, I, abb. 27
ANGEL-(1) WITH WINGS-(2) GLOWING, INSTRUCTING MARY-
BV AND POINTING FINGER-(1) AND HOLDING BANNER.
MARY-BV, STANDING, HOLDING BOOK-(1) AND SHYING-
AWAY, SEEMINGLY AFRAID. POTTED-PLANT BETWEEN
THEM.

11. Crucifixion
c1410–1415
Berlin, German Museum
Seibt, fig. 194a   Matejcek, pl. 147
Stange, II, abb. 76
CHRIST, HALOED, SUFFERING, DRESSED IN LOINCLOTH IS
HANGING AND NAILED TO CROSS-(1) WITH FEET CROSSED,
ARMS-(2) OUTSTRETCHED AND BLEEDING, HIS HEAD IN-

CLINED WITH CROWN-OF-THORNS, AND EYES-HALF-CLOSED, AND CHEST WITH GASH. WOMAN-(1) IS STANDING, SORROWFUL, AND DRESSED IN BLACK-GOWN. MAN-(1) IS STANDING WITH HANDS-(2) UPRAISED, INSPIRED AND COMPASSIONATE, DRESSED IN RED-GOWN.

12. Resurrection from Vyssi Brod Cycle
Meister von Hohenfurth
c1350–1355
Prague, National Gallery
Matejcek, pl. 17   Stange, I, abb. 176, 178
Stange [GP], pl. 45   Stange [DGM], pl. 33
CHRIST, ALL-KNOWING, DRESSED IN WHITE-GOWN AND BAREFOOT, SITTING ON OPEN-CASKET AND LOOKING-STRAIGHT-AHEAD, HOLDING SCEPTRE. SOLDIERS DRESSED IN ARMOR AND HOLDING WEAPON-(1); TWO SITTING SURPRISED AND AFRAID, ONE CROUCHING WITH ARMS-(2) FOLDED ON KNEES. ANGEL-(1) WITH WINGS-(2) SITTING ON CASKET HOLDING CLOTH. WOMEN-(3), EACH DRESSED IN BLACK-GOWN, STANDING AND HOLDING CONTAINER, ADORING.

13. Entombment from Passion Altar
Meister Bertram
1394
Hannover, Landesmuseum
Stange, II, abb. 172
CHRIST, SUFFERING AND DEAD, HALOED AND DRESSED IN LOINCLOTH, CROWN-OF-THORNS, AND WRAPPED IN SHEER-CLOTH, HANDS-(2) BLEEDING WITH GASH IN CHEST, LYING ON OPEN-CASKET. MARY-BV, GRIEVING AND COMPASSIONATE, TOUCHING HAND, WOMEN-(2), HALOED STANDING, LOVING AND CARING. MEN-(2), SAD AND BEARDED, PLACING CHRIST IN CASKET. MAN-(1) WITH CROWN STANDING AND SILENT, HOLDING CONTAINER AND SPOON. ONLOOKERS.

14. God Warns Adam and Eve from Altar of St. Peter
Meister Bertram
c1379
Hamburg, Kunsthalle
Musper, text pl. 36   Lichtwark, s. 203
Platte, tf. 9   Musper [GM], pl. 168
Portmann, tf. 8

GOD, BEARDED, LONG-HAIR, DRESSED IN RED-GOWN, ALL-
KNOWING, POINTING FINGER-(1), WARNING NAKED ADAM
AND NAKED EVE. BOTH STANDING, LISTENING AND INNO-
CENT. ADAM POINTING FINGER-(1) AT FRUITTREE. EVE PAT-
TING STOMACH WITH HAND-(1). TREE-(1) AND ORNATE-
CASTLE WITH OPEN-DOORWAY.

15. Resurrection from Trebon Altar
c1385–1390
Prague, National Gallery
Seibt, pl. VIII   AT, cat. 139, p. 32
VSL, p. 120   Burger, I, tf. XII
Kutal, pl. 115   Matejcek, pl. 96
Simson, fig. 287   Musper [GM], pl. 146
Stange [GP], pl. 55   Stange [DGM], pl. 48
Stange, II, abb. 61
CHRIST, HALOED, ALL-KNOWING, AND DRESSED IN RED-
GOWN, BAREFOOT, STEPPING FROM CLOSED-CASKET; HOLD-
ING SCEPTRE, GASH IN CHEST AND BLEEDING FROM HOLES
IN FEET. SOLDIERS HOLDING WEAPON-(1), SITTING, AFRAID
AND CURIOUS, OR SLEEPING. TREES LINE JAGGED-GROUND;
STARS.

16. Madonna of Veveri
c1350
Prague, National Gallery
Seibt, ill. 91   Matejcek, pl. 26
AT, cat. 133, pl. 22
MARY-BV, SERENE, DRESSED IN ORNATE-GOWN AND CROWN,
HALOED, HOLDING CHRIST-AS-INFANT IN HER ARM-(1), GAZ-
ING OUTWARDS, AND TOUCHING CHRIST'S ARM. CHRIST-AS-
INFANT GAZING, HALOED AND CLUTCHING BIRD-(1) IN
HAND-(1) AND MARY'S SCARF IN THE OTHER.

17. Annunciation
Lubeck Master
c1400
Lubeck, St. Annen Museum
Musper, text pl. 41   Musper [GM], pl. 101
GOD OBSERVANT FROM ABOVE. ANGEL-(1), HALOED, SERENE
WITH WINGS-(2), CROUCHING AND HANDS-(2) CROSSED.
MARY-BV, THOUGHTFUL AND HALOED, WITH HANDS

CROSSED, KNEELING BEFORE LECTERN WITH BOOK-(1). WOMAN-(1) INTENT HOLDING DRAPERY BENEATH CANOPY.

18. Visitation
c1400
Cologne, Wallraf-Richartz

Stange, III, abb. 79	Reiners, abb. 38
VSL, p. 111	Burger, II, abb. 460

MARY-BV AND WOMAN-(1), CALM, SILENT, AND SERENE STANDING BESIDE DOORWAY IN FRONT OF STARS. MARY-BV HALOED, PREGNANT DRESSED IN GREEN-GOWN HOLDING BOOK-(1). WOMAN-(1) HALOED DRESSED IN RED-GOWN REACHING WITH HAND-(1) AND TOUCHING STOMACH OF MARY-BV.

19. Crucifixion from Wildungen Altar
Konrad von Soest
c1403
Wildungen, Evangelischer Kirche

Stange [GP], pl. 67	Burger, II, abb. 487, 492
Glaser, pl. 19	gAN, abb. 18, 23
Steinbart, pl. VIII, ill. 26	Eckert, p. 88
Glaser [AM], pl. 41	Winkler, p. 13
Stange, III, abb. 13	

CHRIST, HALOED, WITH CROWN-OF-THORNS, DRESSED IN LOINCLOTH, SUFFERING, HANGING ON CROSS-(1), NAILED AND BLEEDING. MAN-(1) PIERCING CHEST OF CHRIST WITH SPEAR-(1). CROSS-(1), STANDING-UPRIGHT, WITH PLAQUE ON IT; BONES AND SKULL AT BASE. SAD ANGELS-(4); TWO FLYING, ONE HOLDING CHALICE UP TO CHRIST; ONE WEEPING. KING WITH CROWN, DISINTERESTED TALKING. WOMAN-(1), HALOED, LOVING AND MAN-(1) SITTING, SORROWFUL, WITH BOOK-(1) IN LAP. ELDERLY-MEN-(2) DRESSED IN ORNATE-GOWN; ONE UNFURLING BANNER IN UPRAISED ARM-(1).

20. Annunciation from Passion Altar
Meister Bertram
1394
Hannover, Landesmuseum
Stange, II, abb. 176

MARY-BV, HALOED, SURPRISED, KNEELING AT LECTERN BE-
FORE OPEN-BOOKS-(2), HAND-(1) TOUCHING CHEST, SILENT.
FORCEFUL ANGEL-(1), HALOED, KNEELING, DRESSED IN OR-
NATE-GOWN, HOLDING BANNER, INSTRUCTING WITH FIN-
GER-(1) POINTING, TALKING TO MARY-BV. POTTED-PLANT
ON FLOOR WITH TILES. MAN-(1), OBSERVANT WITH ARM-(1)
OUTSTRETCHED. CHRIST-AS-INFANT AND DOVE-(1) FLYING.
ANGELS-(4), PROTECTIVE, INTERESTED, OBSERVANT FROM
ORNATE-CASTLE WHERE CENSERS-(2) ARE SUSPENDED.

INDEX TO ABBREVIATIONS

abb. = abbildung (plate)

c = circa (approximately)

cat. = catalog

fig. = figure

ill. = illustration

no. = number

p. = page

pl. = plate

pp. = pages

s. = seite (page)

ss. = saints

st. = saint

tf. = tafel (plate)

KEY TO SOURCES OF REPRODUCTIONS

[AT]. *L'Art ancien en Tchécoslovaquie*. Paris: Musée des Arts Decoratifs,
1957.

Burger, Fritz. *Die deutsche Malerei*. Berlin-Neubabelsberg: Akademische
Verlagsgesellschaft, 1913. 3v.

Eckert, Ingeborg. *Ein Altargemälde der Gotik*. Bielefeld: Ceres Verlag,
1956.

[gAN]. *Gotische Altare in Nordhessen*. Kassel: Hessische Druck- und
Verlagsanstalt.

Glaser, Curt. *Les Peintres primitifs Allemands*. Paris: Les Editions G. van
Oest, 1931.

Glaser [AM]. Glaser, Curt. *Die altdeutsche Malerei*. Munich: Verlag von
F. Bruckmann, 1924.

Glaser [ZJdM]. Glaser, Curt. *Zwei Jahrhunderte deutsche Malerei*. Munich:
F. Bruckmann U. G., 1916.

Kutal, Albert. *Gothic Art in Bohemia and Moravia*. New York: Hamlyn,
1971.

Lichtwark, Alfred. *Meister Bertram*. Hamburg: Lutcke and Wulff, 1905.

Matejcek, Antonin, and Pesina, Jaroslav. *Czech Gothic Painting, 1350–
1450*. Melantrich Traha, 1950.

Musper, Heinrich Theodor. *Gotische Malerei nordlich der Alpen*. Cologne:
Verlag M. DuMont Schauberg, 1961.

Musper [AM]. Musper, Heinrich Theodor. *Altedeutsche Malerei*. Cologne: Verlag M. DuMont Schauberg, 1970.

Platte, Hans. *Meister Bertram in der Hamburger Kunsthalle*. Berlin:
Hartmann.

Portmann, Paul. *Meister Bertram*. Zurich: Rabe Verlag, 1963.

Reiners, Heribert. *Die Kölner Malerschule*. M. Gladbach, 1925.

Schiller, Gertrude. *Iconography of Christian Art*. Greenwich, Conn.: New
York Graphic Society, 1968-. 2v.

Seibt, Ferdinand, et al. *Gothic Art in Bohemia*. New York: Praeger, 1977.

Simson, Otto von. *Das Mittelalter II*. Berlin: Propylaen Verlag, 1972.

Stange, Alfred. *Deutsche Malerei der Gotik*. Berlin: Deutscher Kunstverlag, 1934–1960. 11v.

Stange [DGM]. Stange, Alfred. *Deutsche Gotische Malerei*. Konigstein im
Tanaus: Hans Koster, 1964.

Stange [GP]. Stange, Alfred. *German Painting*. New York: Macmillan,
1950.

Steinbart, Kurt. *Konrad von Soest*. Vienna: Anton Schroll, 1946.

[VSL]. *Vor Stefan Lochner: die Kölner Maler von 1300–1430*. Cologne:
Wallraf-Richartz Museum, 1977.

Winkler, Friedrich, *Altdeutsche Tafelmalerei*. Munich: Bruckmann, 1944.

APPENDIX B

Clusters in Context

One example of a cluster in context is provided for each of the five categories of clusters in context interpreted by iconographers.

A. One theme is described by the descriptive phrases of the cluster in context.

B. One identifiable theme predominates in the cluster in context, but descriptive phrases referring to other themes can be singled out.

C. No one theme predominates; descriptive phrases refer to two or more themes.

D. The cluster is context does not convey enough information to describe any theme.

E. The cluster in context does not describe a theme.

```
                           angel-(1) with wings-(2) kneeling before Mary
                           angel-(1) with wings-(2) stepping towards Mary
            angel-(1) holding banner
                           dove-(1) flying into Mary
                           dove-(1) flying into woman-(1)
Mary touching her chest with hand-(1)
                           Mary kneeling at lectern
                           Mary sitting on ornate throne
                           Mary sitting on throne
                           Mary standing at lectern

                           A.
```

Christ kneeling and praying on hill
                    men-(3) sleeping, arms-(2) folded
        elderly man with pouch and key hanging from belt
           Joseph with pouch hanging from belt
               cliff and trees
               hill and trees

B.

---

                    forceful angel-(1) instructing with arm-(1) outstretched
                    forceful angel-(1) instructing with finger-(1) pointing
        Christ sitting on open casket
Christ standing in front of open casket
           Christ holding sceptre
                    soldiers sitting holding weapon
        soldiers sitting surprised

C.

---

        chalice upon hill and jagged ground
            angel-(1) in sky holding banner
            angel-(1) in sky with stars
                    trees
                    trees and cliffs

D.

        Mary and Elizabeth busy, reading and working
            Mary busy, mending shirt
            Mary intent, mending shirt
            Mary intent, reading book-(1)
            Mary observant

E.

References

Ackerman, James S. "Western Art History." In *Art and Archeology*, pp. 123–232. Edited by Rhys Carpenter and James S. Ackerman. Englewood Cliffs, N.J.: Prentice-Hall, 1963.

Acuff, Bette C., and Sieber-Suppes, Joan. "A Manual for Coding Descriptions, Interpretations, and Evaluations of Visual Art Forms." ED 071 991. Palo Alto, Calif.: Stanford University, Center for Research and Development in Teaching, December 1972.

Allen, Rachel M. "Office of Research Support; National Museum of American Art." *Picturescope* 31 (Spring 1984): 72–77.

Atherton, Pauline, and Borko, Harold. "A Test of the Factor-Analytically Derived Automated Classification Method Applied to Descriptions of Work and Search Requests of Nuclear Physicists." New York: American Institute of Physics, 1965.

Bailey, Henry Turner, and Ethel Pool. *Symbolism for Artists: Creative and Appreciative*. Worcester, Mass.: Davis Press, 1925.

Berlyne, D. C., and Ogilvie, J. C. "Dimensions of Perception in Paintings." In *Studies in the New Experimental Aesthetics: Steps toward an Objective Psychology of Aesthetic Appreciation*, pp. 181–226. Edited by D. E. Berlyne. New York: Wiley, 1974.

Betz, Elisabeth W. "Subject Headings Used in the Library of Congress Prints and Photographs Division." Washington, D.C.: Prints and Photographs Division, Library of Congress, 1980.

Bisogni, Fabio. "The 'Catalogue of Italian Art': A Computer-Produced Iconographical Analysis." *Museum* 30 (1978): 199–204.

Cameron, Duncan F., et al. "The Public and Modern Art." *Museum* 22 (1969): 129–47.

Canter, David, "An Intergroup Comparison of Connotative Dimensions in Architecture." *Environment and Behavior* 1 (June 1969): 37–48.

Castonguay, Denis. Vocabulary Control in Iconography at the Public Archives of Canada. In *Data Bases in the Humanities and Social Sciences: Proceedings of the International Federation for Information Processing Society Working Conference on Data Bases in the Humanities and Social Sciences*, pp. 257–61. Edited by Joseph Raben and Gregory A. Marks. Amsterdam: North-Holland, 1980.

Castonguay, Denis. Approche sujet en iconographie Canadienne à l'aide d'un lexique de termes controlés. In *Computerized Inventory Standards for Works of Art*, pp. 269–80. Compiled by Raymond Vezina. Montreal: Editions Fides, 1981.

Chenhall, Robert G. *Nomenclature for Museum Cataloging: A System for Classifying Man-Made Objects*. Nashville: American Association for State and Local History, 1978.

Clifford, H. T., and Stephenson, W. *An Introduction to Numerical Classification*. New York: Academic Press, 1975.

Cormack, R. M. "A Review of Classification." *Journal of the Royal Statistical Society* 134A (1971): 321–67.

Couprie, Leendert D. "Constructing and Editing an Alphabetical Index to the Iconographic Classification System Iconclass with the Aid of Electronic Data-Processing, and a Few Ideas for Future Application of the Stored Data." In *International Conference on Automatic Processing of Art History Data and Documents*, pp. 151–77. Pisa, 1978a.

Couprie, Leendert D. "Iconclass, a Device for the Iconographical Analysis of Art Objects." *Museum* 30 (1978b): 194–98.

Couprie, Leendert D. "Iconclass: An Iconographic Classification System." *Art Libraries Journal* 8 (Summer 1983): 32–49.

Couprie, Leendert D. "Report on Iconclass." Leiden: Department of Art History, University of Leiden, 1984a.

Couprie, Leendert D. "Iconclass: an iconographic classification system." In *Census: Computerization in the History of Art*, 1:232–33. Edited by Laura Corti. Pisa: Scuola Normale Superiore; Los Angeles: J. Paul Getty Trust, 1984b.

Dane, William J. *The Picture Collection Subject Headings*. 6th ed. New York: Shoe String Press, 1968.

Decimal Index to Art of the Low Countries. The Hague: Rijksbureau voor Kunsthistorische Documentaire, 1968.

Diamond, Robert M. "The Development of a Retrieval System for 35mm Slides Utilized in Art and Humanities Instruction; Final Report." ED 031 925. Fredonia, N.Y.: State University of New York, March 1969.

Diamond, Robert M. "A Retrieval System for 35mm Slides Utilized in Art and Humanities Instruction." In *Bibliographic Control of Non-*

print Media, pp. 346–59. Edited by Pearce S. Grove and Evelyn G. Clement. Chicago: American Library Association, 1972.

Drake, Maurice, and Drake, Wilfred. *Saints and Their Emblems*. London: T. Werner Laurie, 1916.

Ferguson, George W. *Signs and Symbols in Christian Art*. New York: Oxford University Press, 1967.

Fink, Eleanor, and Yarnall, James L. "The Slide and Photograph Archives." In *Census: Computerization in the History of Art*, Vol. 1, pp. 286–87. Edited by Laura Corti. Pisa: Scuola Normale Superiore; Los Angeles: J. Paul Getty Trust, 1984.

Firschein, Oscar, and Fischler, Martin A. "A Study in Descriptive Representation of Pictorial Data." AD 734 012. Palo Alto, Calif.: Lockheed Missiles and Space Co., February 1971a.

Firschein, Oscar, and Fischler, Martin A. "Describing and Abstracting Pictorial Structures." *Pattern Recognition* 3 (1971b): 421–43.

Firschein, Oscar, and Fischler, Martin A. "Describing and Abstracting Pictorial Data; Final Report." AD 762 515. Palo Alto, Calif.: Lockheed Missiles and Space Co., 1973.

Glass, Elizabeth, comp. *A Subject Index for the Visual Arts*. London: Her Majesty's Stationery Office, 1969. 2 volumes.

Gombrich, E. H. *Symbolic Images*. London: Phaidon, 1972.

Green, Stanford J. *The Classification and Cataloging of Pictures and Slides*. Denver: Little Books, 1981.

Hartigan, John A. *Clustering Algorithms*. New York: Wiley, 1975.

Heusinger, Lutz. "Marburger Index." In *Papers: Automatic Processing of Art History Data and Documents*, 1:43–62. Edited by Laura Corti. Pisa: Scuola Normale Superiore; Los Angeles: J. Paul Getty Trust, 1984.

Hill, Donna. *The Picture File*, Hamden, Conn.: Linnett Books, 1975.

Index of Christian Art. Princeton, N.J.: Department of Art and Archaeology, Princeton University, 1917-.

Ireland, Norma Olin. *The Picture File in School, College, and Public Libraries*. Boston: F. W. Faxon, 1952.

Irvine, Betty Jo. *Slide Libraries: A Guide for Academic Institutions, Museums, and Special Collections*. 2d ed. Littleton, Colo.: Libraries Unlimited, 1979.

Jardine, Nicholas, and Sibson, Robin. *Mathematical Taxonomy*. New York: Wiley, 1971.

K. G. Saur Incorporated. "Marburger Index: Inventory of Art in Germany." New York: K. G. Saur Incorporated, 1983.

Knox, Katharine McCook. *The Story of the Frick Art Reference Library: The Early Years*. New York: Frick Art Reference Library, 1979.

Lindsay, Kenneth C. "Computer Input Form for Art Works: Problems and Possibilities." In *Computers and Their Potential Applications in Museums*, pp. 19–37. New York: Arno, 1968.

Logan, Anne Marie. "Computerized Indexing of British Art." In *International Conference on Automatic Processing of Art History Data and Documents*, pp. 217–33. Pisa, 1978.

Logan, Anne Marie. "Online Subject Access in the Photographic Archives at the Yale Center for British Art." In *Information Interaction; Proceedings of the American Society for Information Science*, pp. 169–72. Edited by Anthony E. Petrarca, Celianna I. Taylor, and Robert S. Kohn. White Plains, N.Y.: Knowledge Industry Publications, 1982.

Markey, Karen. "Interindexer Consistency Tests: A Literature Review and Report of a Test of Consistency in Indexing Visual Materials." *Library and Information Science Research* 5 (1983): 337–63.

Markey, Karen. "Interindexer Consistency Tests: A Literature Review and Report of a Test of Consistency in Indexing Visual Materials." *Library and Information Science Research* 6 (1984): 155–77.

Mischo, William H. "Expanded Subject Access to Reference Collection Materials." *Journal of Library Automation* 12 (December 1979): 338–54.

National Museum of American Art. "Subject Term Guide." Washington, D.C.: Office of Research Support, National Museum of American Art, 1983.

Ohlgren, Thomas H. "Computer Indexing of Illuminated Manuscripts for Use in Medieval Studies." *Computers and the Humanities* 12 (1978): 189–99.

Ohlgren, Thomas H., ed. *Illuminated Manuscripts: An Index to Selected Bodleian Library Color Reproductions*. New York: Garland Publishing, 1977.

Ohlgren, Thomas H., and Lelvis, Gary C. "The Digital Scriptorium: Computer Indexing of Medieval Manuscripts." *Art and Archeology Research Papers* (December 1973): 149–57.

Osgood, Charles; Suci, George J.; and Tannenbaum, Percy H. *The Measurement of Meaning*. Urbana: University of Illinois, 1967.

Panofsky, Erwin. *Studies in Iconology*. New York: Oxford University Press, 1939; reprint ed., New York: Harper & Row, 1962.

Panofsky, Erwin. *Meaning in the Visual Arts*. Garden City, N.Y.: Doubleday Anchor Books, 1955.

Potter, Eleanor, and Barton, Ruth. "The Picture File of the Fine Arts Department of the Detroit Public Library: A Manual of Procedures and Practices." *Picturescope* 18 (1970): 135–54.

Rocchio, John J., Jr. "Document Retrieval Systems—Optimization and

Evaluation." Report ISR–10. Ph.D. dissertation, Cornell University, 1966.

Salton, Gerard. *Dynamic Information and Library Processing*. Englewood Cliffs, N.J.: Prentice-Hall, 1975.

Salton, Gerard, and Wong, Anita. "Generation and Search of Clustered Files." *ACM Transactions on Database Systems* 3 (December 1978): 321–46.

Sarasan, Lenore. "Visual Content Access: An Approach to the Automatic Retrieval of Visual Information." In *Papers: Automatic Processing of Art History Data and Documents*, 1:387–406. Edited by Laura Corti. Pisa: Scuola Normale Superiore; Los Angeles: J. Paul Getty Trust, 1984.

Sarasan, Lenore, and A. M. Neuner. *Museum Collections and Computers*. Lawrence, Kan.: Association of Systematics Collections, 1983.

Schoenherr, Douglas. "Standards Developed by the Picture Division of the Public Archives of Canada for the Description of Works of Art." In *Computerized Inventory Standards for Works of Art*, pp. 233–60. Compiled by Raymond Vezina. Montreal: Editions Fides, 1981.

Sill, Gertrude. *A Handbook of Symbolism in Christian Art*. New York: Collier Books, 1975.

Simons, Wendell W., and Tansey, Luraine C. "A Slide Classification System for the Organization and Automatic Indexing of Interdisciplinary Collections of Slides and Photographs." ED 048 879. Santa Cruz: University of California, 1970.

Slamecka, Vladimir, and Jacoby, Joan J. "The Consistency of Human Indexing." In *The Coming Age of Information Technology*, pp. 32–56. Edited by Vladimir Slamecka. Bethesda, Md.: Documentation Inc., 1965.

Sneath, Peter, and Sokal, Robert T. *Numerical Taxonomy*. San Francisco: Freeman, 1973.

Sobinski-Smith, Mary Jane. "Standards for Subject Cataloging and Retrieval at the Yale Center for British Art." In *Data Bases in the Humanities and Social Sciences: Proceedings of the International Federation for Information Processing Society Working Conference on Data Bases in the Humanities and Social Sciences*, pp. 233–37. Edited by Joseph Raben and Gregory A. Marks. Amsterdam: North-Holland Publishing Company, 1980.

Sunderland, John. "The Witt Library Getty Project." *Art Libraries Journal* 8 (Summer 1983): 27–31.

Teyssedre, Bernard. "Iconologie: Reflexions sur un concept d'Erwin Panofsky." *Revue philosophique* 154 (July-September 1964): 321–40.

Vance, David. "Identification of Objects." In *Automatic Processing of Art History Data and Documents*, 2:337–51. Edited by Laura Corti. Pisa: Scuola Normale Superiore; Los Angeles: J. Paul Getty Trust, 1984.

Vezina, Raymond. "The Computer: Passing Fad or Thorough-Going Revolution?" *Visual Resources* 1 (Fall-Winter 1980–1981): 204–18.

Vezina, Raymond, comp. *Computerized Inventory Standards for Works of Art*. Montreal: Editions Fides, 1981.

Waal, Hans van de. *Iconclass, an Iconographic Classification System*. Amsterdam and London: North-Holland Publishing, 1974-.

Williams, W. T. "Principles of Clustering." *Annual Review of Ecology and Systematics* 2 (1971): 303–26.

Williamson, Robert Edward. "Real-Time Document Retrieval." Ph.D. dissertation, Cornell University, 1974.

Wittkower, Rudolf. "Interpretation of Visual Symbols in the Arts." In *Studies in Communication*, pp. 109–24. Sir Alfred Jules, et al. London: Martin Secker and Warburg, 1955.

Woodruff, Helen. *The Index of Christian Art at Princeton University*. Princeton, N.J.: Princeton University Press, 1942.

Yale Center for British Art. "Subject Authority Used by the Photographic Archive." New Haven: Photographic Archive, Yale Center for British Art, 1979.

Index

About the Author

KAREN MARKEY, Research Scientist at the OCLC Online
Computer Library Center in Dublin, Ohio, has been involved in
studies investigating computerized subject retrieval and has presented papers on the topic in the United States and Europe. She
is the author of *Subject Searching in Library Catalogs* and articles
in several professional journals.